Benjamin Martin

The wandering pilgrim

Hymns and spiritual songs

Benjamin Martin

The wandering pilgrim
Hymns and spiritual songs

ISBN/EAN: 9783337196547

Printed in Europe, USA, Canada, Australia, Japan

Cover: Foto ©Thomas Meinert / pixelio.de

More available books at **www.hansebooks.com**

THE

...RING PILGRIM:

COMPOSED OF

...nd Spiritual Songs.

...ENJAMIN MARTIN.

Entered according to act of Congress, in the year of our Lord one thousand eight hundred and sixty-eight,

BY BENJAMIN MARTIN,

in the Clerk's office of the District Court of the United States for the Northern District of Ohio.

PREFACE:

I HAVE composed this little work
   For critic eyes to scan;
Perhaps may please some wandering eye,
   Whilst others 't will offend.

Perhaps some brother would suggest
   It is all well enough;
But hadn't we better try to please,
   Than be too plain and rough?

My work compare with the old Book,
   And should not correspond,
When o'er its pages you should look,
   The fault in me abound.

The Bible I will own my guide,
   Whether I stand or fall;
Mysterious Book! its pages hide
   The wisdom of it all.

But grace and truth reveal a God
   In every line we read;
Confirmed by faith and hope assured,
   Awakens from the dead.

'T is there we read our titles clear,
   In rays of great surprise,
To see a smiling God appear,
   Enwrapt in self-disguise.

The sinner thinks he knows it all,
   And feels himself secured,
Until the Lord confirms his fall,
   He turns without a word.

Delights to find a different rout,
   When Jesus' love reveals,
Trav'ling a path he sought not out,
   By art or human skill.

I leave my book for readers now,
   Inspired with love and zeal,
And stand condemned when you do show
   I've penned with iron will.

Yea! critics who pretend to stand
   Upon the written Word,
Should e'er attempt my work condemn,
   I'll own it is the Lord.

My wanderings here and faults I have,
   With imperfection too,
May look like mountains in the eyes
   Of nobler men. Adieu!

ACROSTIC.

BEGIN, my soul, the heavenly theme!
   Encouraged by the Word;
Ne'er may my tongue despite to name
   Jesus, my Sovereign Lord.
Amidst ten thousand setting snares,
   My God will me defend;
In all my troubles and my cares,
   Nigh me He shall attend.

My earliest boyhood days I view,
   Amazing pity shown;
Rather O let me speak Thy praise,
   Together with Thy power.
I choose to tell that Jesus lives
   Near my abiding tower.
      Complete the stanza with two lines
      Is all that I require.

May God indorse my prayer,
   And will for me to stand,
   While angels guide my hand,
   Enclose a golden pen,
And dream of yonder peaceful land,
   Where happiness does roam,
Where lovely flowers will ever bloom,
Where reigns one long eternal noon,
   In heaven our happy home!

                    BENJAMIN MARTIN.

INDEX TO SUBJECTS.

	PAGE.
The Sovereignty and Majesty of God	1
Natural and Supernatural Religion	3
Salvation by Grace	11
The Sufferings of Christ	19
The Church and its Members	21
Christian Trials and Experience	26
Baptism	43
Fellowship	49
Parting Hymn	55
Election and Preservation	56
Judgment Day	67
Death	69
Heaven	78
Morning Devotion	83
Predestination	88
Gifts and Calling	93
Doubts and Fears	103
Love	108
Aaron the Type of Christ	114
Evening Hymn	115
Morning Devotion	116
Sabbath	117
Seasons	118
After Sermon	121
Divine Worship	124
Men's Works Compared with God's	127
Commemoration of the Lord's Supper	139
The Sinner's Friend	142
The Wandering Pilgrim	143
Farewell	250

INDEX OF FIRST LINES.

                                            NO. OF HYMN.

Are there no promises?	122
Ah! once I mourned for sin	37
A song of thankfulness to raise	15
Arise and be baptized	44
A nobleman made a great feast	231
A mighty foe within the breast	64
A gift unto each saint	98
At Zion's hill the pilgrims meet	101
Afflictions are a stormy cloud	184
A monument of mercy	197
And must this body die?	200
Around Thy table, Lord, we come	158
A little hope I have	164
And do I follow Thee?	165
Afflicted, despised	213
A sense, O Lord, of pardoning love	13
Ah! prophecy! who struck thee now?	254
Attend, my soul, upon the Lord	152
Blind, deaf and dumb below	209
By ties of nature and of God	143
Brethren, ye who have the pleasure	144
Baptism is a sacred rite	46
Beneath the gentle wave	47
Brethren, let love now be your aim	55
Brethren, conflicts you must have	110
Behold how pleasant 't is	115
By God's eternal sovereign grace	117
Behold! I see a lady fair	169
By grace the soul is saved	174
But now, says one, what will you do	95

INDEX.

Blest with the smiles of love and peace........ 145
Bless, O my soul, thou God of peace............ 269
Come, children of the Heavenly King.......... 245
Come, humble souls, to Jesus.................. 162
Come, O thou sons of God, proclaim............ 155
Christ, our High Potentate and King.......... 208
Come, all who profess......................... 212
Come, O my friends, remember.................. 216
Come, heavenly tongues, and swell............. 219
Come, tell me, favorites of the Lord............ 27
Can I be a soul possessor?..................... 35
Can such a worthless worm as I................ 38
Come, friends, and tell if e'er you felt......... 52
Come, while your hearts are warm............. 53
Censures we'll gain while dwelling here........ 132
Come, undone and needy sinner................ 135
Come, follow me, my Master cries............. 223
Come, sing to me of heaven.................... 251
Could I but view the eternal love.............. 255
Close by Bethesda's pool....................... 257
Delightful theme, when I can see.............. 247
Dark was the doleful day...................... 207
Dressed, uniformed, the soldiers wear.......... 230
Death is a monster many fear.................. 71
Death, like an overflowing stream............. 69
Death, like an Indian arrow, flies.............. 78
Dear Lord, now tune my harp afresh.......... 173
Dark and doleful was the night................ 262
Endless pleasures now are chiming............. 238
Faith! 't is a precious seed.................... 201
First of all, my friends, I say................. 228
Freed from the pangs of sin and death......... 260
God is a sovereign, reigns on high.............. 1
Great is the Lord, His might excel............. 2
Great God! let men and devils fear............. 5

INDEX.

Give thanks unto the Lord	16
God's law transgressed and yet obeyed	96
Grace like a river flows	253
Gain heaven, I have all things below	202
How should I come before the Lord	239
Heavenly Father, come and reign	241
How sad by nature is our state	140
How will the sons of men appear	141
How could my soul deny the Lord	157
Happy the heart that grace inspires	171
How condescending 't was	195
How dare I knock at mercy's door?	203
Hark! my Redeemer, God	17
Hail! matchless sovereign love that drew	18
Hail! sovereign love that drew the plan	7
How would my heart rejoice to hear	50
How can I bear the word, depart	70
How sweet the blissful hour when first	242
How lonesome and tiresome	211
Heavenly joy awaits the saint	220
How short the race our friend has run	76
How shall I see that happy place	130
Happy the heart where grace inspire	146
How condescending and how kind	150
How can I praise the Lord	107
How solemn yet how fair it is	266
Heavenly dove! celestial spirit!	259
I am weary of life's journey	246
Illustrious day when Jesus shines	206
I must my body soon resign	6
In Isaac do we see portrayed	4
I should the waters tread	48
In Zion, City of our God	62
In that bright world, so far away	67
I've come to the place	80

INDEX.

I will arise when Jesus calls	90
If heaven be thus, O glorious Lord	92
I am a stranger here	100
In darkness once our souls were led	106
In the bright world of endless bliss	114
I will before Jehovah bow	116
In the world that's far away	136
I am a wanderer here below	163
In Judea lies the Babe	175
It is religion to my soul	189
I love to dream of pleasant lands	194
I'm on my journey home	85
I shall praise my God to-day	65
I will advance an idea	229
I must this volume close	275
In every thing befalls us here	264
It doth not yet appear	224
In Thee, O Lord, I put my trust	136
Jesus, the author of my faith	36
Jesus, I love Thy charming name	149
Jesus, with all His servants	233
Jesus, Thy charming name	236
Jesus wept! what solemn feeling	237
Jesus, Thy loving name adored	221
Jesus is the name adored	214
Let every one that knows the Lord	190
Let wolves and lions howl around	66
Let sinners watch and groan and pray	68
Lord, I desire with Thee to live	102
Let sinners rage and men defame	205
Lord, in the morning Thou shalt hear	126
Lord, bless the assembly waiting here	137
Lord, revive my lingering hope	225
Let all our tongues and all our thoughts	263
Let all creation bring	265

INDEX.

Man, subject to temptation's power	3
May we in dust and ashes weep	111
My early life, my boyhood days	120
Man's fall esteems him dignified	187
May we in sweet devotion join	138
My days on earth, O may I spend	154
Matchless and wise Jehovah is	192
'Mid scenes of sorrow	256
My troubles, like a darkened cloud	271
Now let these words suffice to know	240
Nearer to our home above	142
Now let us all unite to praise	161
Now let us all depart in peace	131
Now, brethren, take courage in God	112
Ne'er by the sense of human wit	108
Now, Lord, I do desire to live	11
O solemn day, my heart inspire	235
O ye sinners in the tomb	217
O bless the Lord, ye sinners, now	10
O what a glorious theme to be	14
O may the star that rules Thy Church	24
O would it please the Lord to inspire	25
O what a joyful season 't was	31
O God of truth and love	32, 139
O teach me what I am	39
O come away, my thoughts	42
O may these gentle waters	49
O bless the Lord, my soul, rejoice	51
O what a worthless worm am I	60
O youth, the spark of life's gone down	72
O Thou art gone whom we esteemed	74
O come, come away	88
O what a happy theme	104
O may Thy children, O our God	86
O happy place where Jesus reigns	81

INDEX.

Salvation sent to dying man.................... 252
The truth it is mighty......................... 222
The keenest sense to man is given.............   9
The enemy does try............................ 12
The Church a building art..................... 21
The Zion of our God........................... 22
The Church in full prosperity................. 23
The Church is called a safe retreat........... 26
The Lord holds the screen..................... 30
The Lord, my strength and hope................ 40
The Lord has mercy and is good................ 41
The children of the kingdom here.............. 58
Thou art my God, and Thee I praise............ 29
To praise the Lord a sweet employ............. 31
There's many ways proposed.................... 43
This earthly house must fall.................. 57
There is much said of late.................... 63
The dying saint is heard to say............... 75
To thee, my friend, it does appear............ 77
The Lord is called the sinner's friend........ 83
There is a heaven above....................... 84
The rising sun reminds me now................. 87
The joys we feel are but a taste.............. 28
There is a place below the sky................ 89
Thy hand, great God, unknown to us............ 94
The shadows of one night...................... 97
Thy ways are ways of pleasantness............. 103
There is a way for pilgrims here.............. 121
There is a dwelling for the good.............. 123
There is a place where Jesus reigns........... 159
This day is set apart......................... 127
The changing season tells us.................. 129
They led him forth to Calvary's brow.......... 166
This is a day in which our prayers............ 168
There is a sound in heavenly climes........... 172

xiv INDEX.

O how blest the sister bereft	79
O now, my gracious God	113
Once in my time I started out	54
Our under shepherd, husband, friend	73
Our fathers ignorant were	93
One more day does now expire	125
O how refreshing is the rain	128
O God of truth and love	139
O bless the Lord, my soul	151
On Calvary's mount a river runs	156
O may I ever find	160
O, spotless Lamb of God	176
O what is life, with all her joys	188
O Lord, I will Thy name extol	179
O Jesus! lover of my soul	182
On Jordon's banks the Baptist stood	45
Our meeting here has been	56
O heavenly spirit! come	258
Pierced me, ye railing sinners stood	167
Preserve me, Lord, for in Thy name	198
Peter's faith away it gave	109
Permit now, dear brother	91
Praises to our Intercessor	59
Religion, O what faults are there	8
Religion is the only theme	170
Religion, how divine	267
Should I please, with pleasant speech	218
Shall the Lord again appear	243
Such matchless love as this	177
Sweet was the time when first I knew	178
Salvation, O melodious sound	119
Send forth Thy great, victorious arm	105
Some thousand years or more ago	20
Salvation, 't is my greatest theme	33
Sweet flowers of Paradise	274

There is a day of pure delight.................. 180
The Church adorned with grace................ 181
The powers of man or angels can.............. 185
There is a hope, a blissful hope.................. 191
There is a heaven above the sky............... 193
There is a house for weary souls............... 196
The Bible proves a sealed book.................. 199
The soul that loves is born of God............. 148
There is a way to men seems right............ 153
The voice of the turtle............................. 250
There is a period known to God................ 270
The cause of heaven............................... 273
Toiling and rowing here.......................... 204
Unite my roving thoughts....................... 118
Vain are our trifling joys below................ 210
Vain, delusive world, adieu..................... 215
Vain world, begone, with all your joys........ 147
When Jesus shall appear again................. 183
Who can withstand the powers of God?...... 186
When I look back my life to read.............. 226
When I survey the wondrous cross............ 134
Why is it thus with me, O Lord?............... 133
When Aaron in the holiest went............... 124
What strong cementing ties..................... 82
Why was I made to hear Thy voice?........... 61
Why was it Adam fell?........................... 227
What worthless worms are we.................. 232
Weary and sore distressed....................... 244
When shall I see my Saviour's face............ 248
What charming words from Jesus flow........ 249
What wandering minds to rove................. 261
Who is the Prince of Peace?..................... 268
What charming thoughts compose............. 272
When in my youthful days...................... 99
Yea, blessed day when first the Lord.......... 234

The Wandering Pilgrim.

HYMN 1.   C. M.

THE SOVEREIGNTY AND MAJESTY OF GOD.

1 GOD is a sovereign, reigns on high,
   All-wise and just and true,
Creator of all things, even I,
   To whom all praise is due.

2 He formed the deep and gave their bound,
   And filled with waters o'er
This earth and all her solid ground,
   Her costly diamonds too.

3 O, who is like Thee! Mighty God,
   Whose voice can stop Thy hand?
Thou say'st 'tis done even with a word,
   We quake at the command.

4 'Tis in Thee we live and move,
   And have our being here;
Thy blessings crown us when we sow,
   And brings the reaping year.

5 Let beggars, kings and mighty men,
   Thy matchless power adore;
While saints attempt to praise Thy name,
   May sinners tremble too.

NO. 2. L. M.

1 GREAT is the Lord, His might excel
  The power of human skill to tell,
  His eye is over what He's done,
  With firm decrees the work begun.

2 The earth's foundation is obscure,
  While ancients pried with all their power,
  The wits of modern men have found,
  A place where is no solid ground.

3 The land and sea, their bounds are made,
  The sun and moon around them wade;
  Though surges roll, though tumults rise
  They're governed by the Great All-Wise.

4 The work of life, the God of skill,
  'Tis too profound the seraphs hail;
  Man in the image of his God,
  The Captain of his works to plaud.

5 The angels hail their sovereign God,
  While he pronounce the work is good,
  Appoints a day of sacred rest,
  To be observed by all the blest.

NO. 3. L. M.

1 MAN, subject to temptation's power,
  Deceived himself in one lone hour—
  Brought his posterity to die
  Degraded, fell in misery.

2 But by the fall it was ordained
Should rise a nation great and strong,
Unto the woman typified,
To Abram was it verified.

3 But man condemned by the law,
Its precepts then began to draw,
How shall he now his state reclaim
And God be just in his demand.

4 Here's wisdom too profound for me,
God's law shall ever honored be,
And yet he shall a people save,
There names be honored in the grave.

5 This God that made the worlds hath said,
In Isaac shall my fame be made,
And lying on the altar there,
A type of one he should prepare.

NO. 4.   L. M.

1 IN Isaac do we see portrayed,
When on the altar he was laid,
An offering needs must be made,
God in his wisdom did provide.

2 The chosen sons of Israel,
On one lone brother what befell,
Cast in the pit, raised up and sold,
Proved them a saviour, a stronghold.

3 The law of God to them renewed,
In solemn awe the promise viewed,
So long ye keep this covenant
I shall be found throughout your tent.

THE WANDERING PILGRIM.

4 To bless and sanctify your cause,
   And cause obedience to my laws,
   In all His works we see His hand,
   In blessing them in Canaan's land.

5 In all their sacrifices made,
   We see one typified;
   The appointed priest their gifts assumed,
   The sons of Israel presumed.

6 While Aaron once a year repaired
   The holiest with His breast-plate marred,
   With all the tribes of Israel,
   It typified Emanuel.

7 The prophets freely spoke of Him
   That in a latter day should come
   The order of Melchisedec,
   A royal priesthood should set up.

8 This Priest has come, Jesus our Lord,
   The Holy Writ has been made good,
   Honored the law of Israel's God,
   By pouring out His vital blood.

9 While on his breast-plate was portrayed,
   The names of all the sons of God;
   Their condemnation in the fall
   Was sanctified in days of old.

10 Jesus now stands between the twain—
   Offended God, offending man;
   But lo! we lay in nature's night,
   And deaf to God and deaf to right!

11 How shall their safety be made known,
Has puzzled kings upon the throne;
How is it done, can we agree,
Some say by faith, O, let me see!

12 Faith, faith! O, precious gift, what bestowed,
I read it is the gift of God;
O, God of heaven, how can it be
We've got to trust the whole to Thee!

13 Thy hand can bring the noble down,
The loftiest monarch on the throne!
The beggar raise to wear a crown,
With scepters of a mighty king!

NO. 5. L. M.

1 GREAT God, let men and devils fear,
With august reverence to Thee bow,
In one short blow thy arm befell
Can sink whole nations down to hell!

2 With Thee, the nations rise and fall,
Thy law upholds and fixes all;
With sins oppressed men turn apace
And seek Thee through Thy sovereign grace.

3 Their time is fixed and written stand
When they shall turn and seek Thy hand,
While all the powers of earth combined
Can't change one title of Thy mind.

4 How solemn then our case does lie
Without one hope to reach the sky,
Unless the God of heaven sees fit
To raise us from the miry pit.

5 The God of heaven inspires with hope,
  To those He choose to raise them up,
  While they acknowledge through His name,
  Their faith and their repentance came.

NO. 6.   S. M.

1 I MUST my body soon resign,
  Where savages and mighty men,
  The beggars in the dungeon bred,
  Will join with kings on dainties fed,
  Around one common resting place
  Resign our bodies to His grace,
  Who'll call us to the judgment bar,
  And there our formal sentence hear.

2 Without distinction, color, race,
  Some will arise to see His face,
  And others sink beneath a frown.
  Earth's dignities can't wear a crown
  While men of meaner birth receive
  The pard'ning news, arise to live!
  Where kings and priest with mighty men
  With beggars on one common stand.

3 God's justice is in what He's done,
  Man to restore He sent His Son,
  The law remitting blood was shed,
  'Twas only for the present deed.
  While Jesus once for us obeyed,
  The unctions of the law was stayed,
  And while the law the sinner slays
  He looks to Jesus Christ and lives.

4 Now if He should in justice see
  Fit to save one sinner like me,

And others run quite heedless on,
Can God be blamed for crimes I've done?
If He sees fit to let me run
I have no claim upon His Son,
Only through mercy can I plea,
Forgiveness through His Son to me.

5 Or if He should some others save
And let me sink beneath the wave,
How can I claim a partial God,
Without I can my case applaud,
Most surely He is just and right,
To send me down to darkest night,
But this will stand my urgent plea,
In mercy, Lord, remember me.

NO. 7.   L. M.

1 HAIL Sovereign love that drew the plan,
To rescue lost and fallen man.
'Twas made so strong, so manned with skill,
'Tis safe without the creature's will.

2 To Abram was the promise made,
In thee and even to thy seed,
With wisdom shall the blessing greet,
To worship at Emanuel's feet.

3 This blessing shall Messiah make good,
And seal it with his precious blood,
While Abram's seed the blessing greet,
To worship at Emanuel's feet.

4 O, countless race, O blessed God,
A people saved by the Lord,
How glorious is thy safe retreat,
To worship at Emanuel's feet.

5 Down through all time a race shall know
His grace, His will and wisdom too,
Return to Zion their retreat,
And worship at Emanuel's feet.

6 O, can I find within this race,
My lineage trace by sovereign grace,
And find in Thee a safe retreat,
To worship at Emanuel's feet.

NO. 8.   C. M.

NATURAL AND SUPERNATURAL RELIGION.

1 RELIGION! Oh what faults are there,
  Within thy lovely name,
The old, the young, thy cloak do wear,
  A heavenly garment claim.

2 While in appearances we judge,
  They did possess the same,
But nature should not e'er begrudge
  Them of their noble aim.

3 From Boston's hill to New Orleans
  These temples do aspire;
These costly mansions may be seen,
  Ascend the skies their spires.

4 Within these mansions move a throng
  With their religious garb;
From Beecher down we hear the song
  That they applaud the Lord.

5 By works they claim they have the power
  To turn to Zion's hill,

THE WANDERING PILGRIM.

And seek the Lord from that good hour,
And all his precepts fill.

6 They sound their notes from India's shore
   To other foreign lands,
Awaking all the nations o'er,
   Their happiness to wand.

7 Through them the heathen do rejoice,
   To hear the glorious news
That their poor souls can have the choice,
   And hail, King of the Jews.

8 And by their money and their means
   The world will soon commend
To hold free agents in their claims,
   And all the rest condemn.

9 I do not now much hesitate,
   Or dare I to disdain
How many systems meditate,
   His argument proclaim.

10 I do not say my friends are clear
   With whom profession make,
As in the following lines appear,
   It may our centre shake.

11 Some think predestinarians are
   The sons of Israel,
Whilst others think their doctrine far
   Worse than the deepest hell.

12 There's something curious in their speech,
   I can't account for all;
God's wisdom they do claim to preach,
   And leave their own to fall.

13 Can it be possible they would
    Travel both far and wide,
And trust their cares unto their God,
    For their support and guide.

14 I am amazed to hear them tell,
    What their poor souls deserved,
Far greater than the lowest hell;
    But God had still preserved.

15 But after all I cannot see
    Where all their misery lay,
As good as others 'pear to be
    Who are pretenders too.

16 They preach that God'll save his delight,
    And leave the rest to die,
Whilst others preach He would save all,
    If they would come and buy.

17 They claim they have'nt wherewith to pay,
    But trust in Jesus' blood,
While others claim can work their way
    And reconcile their God.

18 They claim that God has made the choice,
    And called them by His grace,
Eternity, thunders His voice,
    Not one shall lose the place.

19 So follows, God chose part or all,
    I dare not now deny,
And not one chosen shall e'er fall,
    But reign above the sky.

20 Whilst others preach God cannot see
    One inch before his face,

And all that will, can ever fee,
  And seek themselves a place.

21 'Tis like unto pre-emption's right,
  You've got to hold your place;
  To keep your claim must be in sight,
  So follows, falls from grace.

22 Now if one soul can ever fall,
  It would God's wisdom vie;
  If one, it follows so may all,
  And God dishonored be.

23 Like Baalam I would choose to die;
  Like Israel may I live;
  The God above to glorify,
  With all the powers I have.

24 For right and justice I contend,
  The Scriptures justify,
  Though hard they are to understand,
  The Lord must qualify.

25 And if my friends can ever find
  One place we've got a choice,
  I'll give up I'm both deaf and dumb,
  And void of every grace.

NO. 9.   C. M.

SALVATION BY GRACE.

1 THE keenest sense to man is given
  By nature can't reveal,
  The grace of God that reigns in heaven,
  Our Father holds the seal.

2 The mighty God of earth and skies,
  Unto the soul impart
  A token from the Great All-Wise
  That makes a change of heart.

3 When once this grace shines in the heart,
  It shows a sink of sin,
  A heart that's treasured with deceit
  That long has wallowed in.

4 Grace slays self-will and gives a will
  Despising every sin,
  And gives a heart to know and feel,
  'Tis grace that saves the man.

5 Where is the saint but what can say,
  I know it's all of grace;
  Grace found me in the downward way,
  And gave what I possess.

NO. 10. C. M.

SALVATION BY GRACE.

1 O BLESS the Lord, ye sinners now,
  For grace and hope and peace,
  While love sits smiling on thy brow,
  Think who the giver is.

2 Jesus the God adorned with love,
  What sufferings he endured,
  Think, O my soul, thy sins did move,
  And caused the swelling flood.

3 Love caused his blood in torrents flow
  On Calvary's bleeding cross,
  His pity now to sinners show
  That he sustained no loss.

4 The reconciliation made
  Wherein we stood condemned,
Behold us reconciled to God,
  And hope and love confirmed.

NO. 11.   C. M.

1 NOW Lord, I do desire to live
  Anew from day to day,
Since grace has taught my soul to love,
  And brought me in the way.

2 Grace found me wallowing in my sin,
  I thought that all was well,
But Oh! what should my case have been,
  Fast sinking down to hell.

3 His grace shall crown my following days
  On earth I have to spend,
To lisp my great Redeemer's praise
  That is in heaven begun.

NO. 12.   S. M.

1 THE enemy does try
  A thousand forms to chase,
Afright my soul that it should die,
  And fall from living grace.

2 But God, whose powerful arm,
  Hath brought salvation down,
Will guard me safe from present harm,
  And safe from harm to come.

NO. 13.   C. M.

1 A SENSE, O Lord, of pard'ning love,
  Reveals the Son of God,

Reforms the creature now to live
In life, in deed and word.

2 Removes the indifferent heart of stone,
And gives a heart of flesh,
A heart despising every sin,
Supplied by living grace.

3 O, teach me, Lord, this grace to feel,
That I may grow thereby,
Restrain me from the sinner's zeal,
That in gross darkness lie.

NO. 14.   C. M.

1 O, WHAT a glorious theme to be
A saint, to live and die;
Grace, like an overflowing stream,
Shall all his wants supply.

2 Although the world may think it strange,
They do so often meet,
And act as if they were deranged
While at the mercy seat.

3 The world can't taste the joys they feel,
Nor what this grace afford,
Saints, to your hearts I will appeal
Before you knew the Lord.

4 The world is blind, so once were we,
Till grace did make us whole;
Grace opened our eyes that we might see,
And did the news unfold.

5 Grace brought us from the mire and clay,
And placed us on the rock,

A sure foundation in that day
For all the ransom flock.

6 Grace in our last expiring breath
Will save us, though we die,
And grace will sing, come welcome death,
I'll gladly go with thee.

7 And in the morning when we wake,
By grace shall see the Lamb,
Who from before this earth was laid,
Was for his chosen slain.

8 We then shall hear the welcome news,
Come to the glorious feast;
Forever sing, forever praise,
The song will be free grace.

NO. 15.   L. M.

1 A SONG of thankful to raise,
And speak of my Redeemer's praise;
His loving kindness, O, how free,
To save a sinner lost like me.

2 Beyond man's reach my soul to save,
Fast traveling onward to the grave,
Arrested me in folly's sin,
And showed what a lost state was in.

3 And at the end of law was lost,
Unless was saved by sovereign grace;
This grace he showed was rich and free
To save a sinner lost like me.

4 Now let my lips expand and tell,
My Jesus hath done all things well;

His grace my every wants supply,
To save a sinner lost like me.

5 I love His cause, I love His name,
O, may it be my only theme
To speak his love and worth so free,
To save a sinner lost like me.

6 When the dark shades of death appear,
Surround this mortal body here,
Will then as now appear as free,
To save a sinner lost like me.

7 When Gabriel's trumpet loud shall blow,
The sinner saved by grace shall know;
Jesus will call, my child arise,
And mount the great and lofty skies.

8 I then shall see and quickly know
From whence this grace so rich does flow,
While seraphs' wings shall bear me way,
Where, O how sweet, this grace will be.

NO. 16.   S. M.

1 GIVE thanks unto the Lord,
    And praise His holy name,
Ye chosen seed of Israel,
    Your Savior's grace proclaim.

2 Sing of His mighty power
    That mortals cannot bound;
His precincts too profound for they
    Who stand nearest His throne.

3 His mercy, like his power,
    Proclaimed to Adam's race,

Unraveling mysteries every hour
By our Redeemer's grace.

4 The worlds He framed by power,
Commands them at His will,
He made the mighty man of war,
The righteous and the ill.

5 Each destined to his place,
Another cannot fill,
Whilst some are chosen by His grace
His pleasure to fulfill.

6 Who art thou? Mighty God,
That holds the destined day,
Who is my Savior, I applaud,
And shows his love to me.

7 Thy grace with glory shine,
Bestowed on rebels here,
In accents sweet with joy divine,
How solemn, yet how fair.

NO. 17.   S. M.

1 HARK, my Redeemer God,
Unveils His fame below,
Where faith and hope and love abounds,
Celestial fruit will grow.

2 A deep and mellow soil,
Prepared by God's own care,
Without the means of human toil,
The fruit of grace appears.

3 Jehovah's plans are deep
Laid in Eternity;

1*

'Twill take Eternity to tell
His grace and majesty.

4 But comely nature smiles
And well adorns the man,
While grace and wisdom ever fills
His heart with love within.

5 O let this wisdom shine
On my poor nature here,
'Twill fit me for declining age,
To worship in Thy fear.

6 'Twill make me fit for heaven,
With all the ransom blest,
Where all my sorrows will be driven
Far from my peaceful breast.

NO. 18. L. M.

1 HAIL! matchless sovereign love, that drew
The great redemption plan,
To save poor wretched sinners, through
The sin atoning Lamb.

2 The spotless Lamb, for sinners slain,
In whom no guile portrayed,
By God's almighty hand proclaimed,
On Him our guilt was laid.

3 He bore the weighty load of all
The chosen family,
In ancient times, in days of old,
And nailed it to the tree.

4 Dire justice fell on Jesus's head,
The spotless Son of God,

That guilty sinners, such as I,
From justice might be freed.

5 What love, amazing love was this
When Jesus bore the stroke,
To raise us to a heavenly bliss,
And all our sorrows took.

6 Dear Lord, how can we e'er repay,
Such gratitude as this?
Call forth our thoughts with humble zeal,
To spread Thy glorious praise.

NO. 19.   C. M.

THE SUFFERINGS OF CHRSIT.

1 LORD, I desire with Thee to live
Since Thou hast made me free,
With tongues of angels canst not tell
How rich Thy treasures be.

2 I was a bondsman, bound in chains,
But Christ has made me free,
He paid the great redemption price,
Upon the accursed tree.

3 He bore my sins, a galling load,
When justice did demand,
To slay Thee, O, my Savior, God,
For me, O, sinful man!

4 Nothing but love e'er brought Him down
To suffer here below;
To bear the scoffs of wicked men,
Salvation to bestow.

THE WANDERING PILGRIM.

NO. 20.   L. M.

1 SOME thousand years or more ago,
   They crucified our Lord, you know;
   Before Judge Pilate's Jewish bar,
   His vile accusers mocked Him there.

2 We still behold their sporting air,
   As though their sins help nail Him there;
   While Christians meet to sing and pray,
   And sing the song, He died for me.

3 The greatest song they ever heard,
   Since first they're brought to know the Lord;
   His grace so rich, so kind and free,
   That each can say, He died for me.

4 It was a Father's feeling love
   That brought Him down from heaven above,
   To hang upon the accursed tree,
   That each can sing, He died for me.

5 While here on earth 'gainst powers combined,
   He marked the road for us to climb;
   Lo! then they hung Him on the tree,
   That each can say, He died for me.

6 An emblem of His power to save,
   They laid Him in Joseph's new grave,
   On the third day His saints did see,
   O, what a thought! He rose for me.

7 Triumphant o'er His enemies,
   Flew to His courts above the skies;
   O'er death and hell you plainly see,
   Each saint can sing, He rose for me.

NO. 21.   S. M.

THE CHURCH AND ITS MEMBERS.

1 THE Church, a building here,
   Secured by God on high,
Its members are renewed in heart,
   By grace from day to day.

2 This building, built on Christ,
   The rock of sure defense;
He says it shall forever stand
   Secured at his expense.

3 The price of blood it cost
   More precious than of beast;
The Lamb of God by sinners slain,
   And they the invited guest.

4 More precious than of gold,
   Or things that will decay,
But O, this feast will ne'er grow old,
   Nor ever fade away!

5 Though subjects here must die,
   And leave the Church below,
Forever shall they reign on high
   Where love like waters flow.

6 No poisonous breath shall rise,
   To cause affliction there;
But perfect love will cheer their skies
   In that great noted day.

NO. 22.   C. M.

1 THE Zion of our God,
　Composed of members here,
Built up in faith and grace and hope,
　E'er to her courts repair.

2 These bring their sacred vows,
　To one another give,
Supported by their God who knows
　Their utmost wants relieve.

3 They're planted here below
　To scent the church with grace,
'Ere soon transplanting God will do,
　Within His blest embrace.

4 Then shall their graces shine
　Like diamonds in the sky,
One brilliant noon-day's beaming sun,
　Shall mid-night hours defy.

5 Shall I be there to see
　The glory of that dawn,
My soul is lost in ecstacy,
　While gazing on the morn.

6 Give o'er my earthen home,
　I can no longer stay,
Come! O my Heavenly Father come,
　And take my soul away.

NO. 23.   C. M.

1 THE Church in full prosperity
　Again I wish to see;
New hopes and cords their appendage be,
　And care-worn thought might flee.

2 Each brother in his place to fill,
    And pleasantly there say :
  I to my brother wish no ill
    While in these courts I stay.

3 But while much ill in us abounds
    We can't expect to see,
  While trav'ling o'er these heavenly grounds
    In fellowship to be.

4 Unless we feel a willing part
    Each brother's faults to hide,
  And pray the Lord with thankful heart,
    We must be still denied.

5 O, then like Israel of old,
    May our petitions rise ;
  For grace and hope our spirits hold ;
    Our prayers ascend the skies.

6 To bring our Great Redeemer nigh,
    And melt the frozen heart ;
  Then pleasantly each brother say,
    All earthly fears depart.

7 Then like the psalmist we could say,
    How pleasant 'tis below,
  When sisters, brothers, all agree ;
    Nothing but love to know.

8 'Tis like the oil on Aaron's head,
    Our great high priest, I know ;
  His graces on the body shed,
    And banishes our woe.

9 'Tis then we here forget our pains
    Almost our sorrows too,

And long to see the heavenly plains
Where none but Jesus know.

10 My soul would gladly now arise
At the great noted day;
Welcome the monarch of the skies,
My God and Savior too.

NO. 24.   C. M.

1 O, MAY the star that rules Thy Church
Once more shine bright and fair,
To sing our Great Redeemer's praise,
While we his mercies share.

2 There's none that knows but Thee, O Lord,
The trials we endure;
Our hope still hovering on Thy word,
That shows Thy mercies sure.

3 Would Thou send forth Thy gracious aid,
And cause Thy Church to rise;
Rise from those transitory things,
To things above the skies.

4 O, may those fiends that mar us now
Forever be removed,
And all thy saints before Thee bow,
To spread a Savior's love.

5 May stubborn hearts repentance bring,
To show their sins forgiven,
E'er sing that great celestial song,
That's carried on in heaven.

NO. 25.   C. M.

1 O, WOULD it please the Lord to inspire
   My heart with love, I pray,
   To run the Christian road, nor tire
   With travels by the way.

2 In all things may I prove sincere,
   Here on the heavenly road,
   Without a hindrance interfere,
   For I have seen the Lord.

3 O, bless the Zion of our cause,
   With merits from Thy store,
   That she may stand the trying hour,
   Her God and King adore.

4 Although her faith is tried with fire,
   Shall her foundation stand,
   And all her sons where'er they die,
   Arise at Thy right hand.

NO. 26.   P. M.

1 THE Church is called a safe retreat
   For all the sons of God,
   And howling foes around may beat,
   And cry they will the host defeat,
   But shall not be dismayed.

2 Her walls like bulwarks stand secure
   Against the host of hell.
   Her inmates are all chosen men,
   Whose armor can't at least be seen
   Without the citadel.

3 Her trumpet gives a certain sound
    For peace, and also war;
  Each member when the trumpet's blown
  Immediately to them's known
    Which way the tidings bear.

4 O, what a glorious hiding place
    Is perched within her tower,
  Where all the chosen sons of grace
  Can rest secure from furious beast,
    And Satan's men of war.

5 O, may I stand within her wall,
    There rest my wearied limbs,
  And patiently await my all
  When Gabriel's trumpet loud shall
    Blow for all her tried ones.

6 Her chosen sons shall soon arise
    For nobler joys above,
  Where sorrows never dark their skies,
  And God shall wipe all weeping eyes
    In smiles of 'lasting love.

NO. 27.

CHRISTIAN TRIALS AND EXPERIENCE.

1 COME, tell me, favorites of the Lord,
    The way to Zion's hill,
  For I have got an aching void
    The world can never fill.

2 My sins oppress and fears surmount
    The comforts of the way;

Come tell me, is it thus with you,
　Old pilgrims, now I pray?

I would delight to hear you tell
　How it has been with you,
If such temptations e'er befell
　Old pilgrims here below.

Your songs and prayers are my delight,
　In which I do rejoice,
Believing you've been taught aright,
　By the great powers of grace.

NO. 28.　　C. M.

1 THE joys we feel are but a taste
　Of those in heaven begun,
Welcome invites us to the feast
　Of God's beloved Son.

2 Perplexed with trials and with cares,
　Which makes us oft repine,
'Tis then we weep with flowing tears,
　And pray and weep again.

3 We often wish ourselves away
　To that bright world of bliss,
Where saints shall reign in endless day,
　In perfect love and peace.

NO. 29.　　C. M.

1 THOU art my God, and Thee I'll praise
　From every setting sun,
Morning and noon my voice I'll raise
　High to the Father's throne.

2 The Lord will hear my great complaints,
   And teach me how to pray;
 And praise my Saviour with His saints
   While in His courts I stay.

3 O'er hills and vales and mountains too,
   Life's rugged ways must go;
 Even still I will my tribute pay,
   While trav'ling here below.

4 And in the morning, high, O God,
   My voice to Thee I'll raise;
 More free and clear, and sweeter, too,
   My tongue shall lisp Thy praise.

5 On harps of gold I shall proclaim
   The Lord's forever King,
 And in the music of Thy name,
   Thy ransom power I'll sing.

6 No chilling winds or poisonous breath
   Shall fright my soul away;
 In perfect love, and peace and health,
   Shall reign in endless day.

NO. 30.   P. M.

1 THE Lord holds the screen,
   And will thoroughly purge his floor—
 Purge out those come in
   By all ways but the door;
 Professors grow tall,
   Like Lebanon cedars;
 Some count them as great
   And audible leaders.

THE WANDERING PILGRIM.

2 And in our affliction
    They give way like dew,
And leave all the saints,
    And yet deceive a few.
Though strong we have stood,
    Well united together,
The Lord in his judgment
    Our union shall sever.

3 There's some will rejoice,
    And some will lament;
This writ we will find
    In the New Testament;
Ye saints now prepare,
    And stand for the truth;
The Lord be with all,
    Ye aged and youth.

4 There is honor in war
    As well as in peace,
If thoroughly invested
    And settled by grace.
Together can't live,
    Unless we agree
In points of doctrine
    And grace, which is free.

5 And in our profession
    We verily believe
The Lord in his wisdom
    Does teach us to love;
But in our compassion
    Have thrown doors too wide,
While some have crept in
    And our liberty spied.

6 In trouble and grief
   They cause us to fear;
The work of the Devil
   Is sure raging here.
Now all who feel bound
   In the doctrine to stand,
Be firm to the cause,
   For the hour is at hand.

7 Even that your faith will
   Be well tried by fire,
And all who're not firm
   Will be shaken with fear—
Be sifted as wheat
   To clean out the chaff;
The Lord holds the screen,
   And He will thoroughly sift.

NO. 31. C. M.

1 O, WHAT a joyful season 'twas
   When first I knew the Lord;
My heart in rapture traced His laws,
   With joy received the word.

2 Alas, the tempter soon proclaimed,
   You're a deceived soul;
I thought, I plead, ne'er had I named,
   None of my vision told.

3 But soon the cloud passed o'er my head,
   The Son in glory shown,
Amid ten thousand stars appeared
   The brightness of His name.

4 O, could I taste such joys once more,
   As in those days gone by;
   So pure a light to mark the way
   That leads above the sky.

5 But now my joyful scenes are few,
   My hope grows dim and faint;
   O tell me, is it thus with you,
   Who is esteemed a saint?

NO. 32.   S. M.

1 O, GOD of truth and love,
   O teach me how to pray,
   And pray in faith, of joys to come
   Of that immortal day.

2 I am a stranger, Lord,
   A wanderer here below,
   And what I am I find 'tis hard
   On earth for me to know.

3 Sometimes I feel inclined
   To love Thee, if I could,
   But often feel another mind
   Averse to all that's good.

4 Incline me more and more
   To love Thee, Lord, I pray,
   And constantly Thy name adore
   While in this mortal clay.

5 And when this body die,
   Receive my soul at rest,
   With all Thy ransomed host on high,
   With Thee forever blest.

NO. 33. C. M.

1 SALVATION, 'tis my greatest theme,
  A comfort to my soul,
This earth with all its arts combined,
  Its beauties can't unfold.

2 A balm to heal the sin-sick soul,
  Speaks peace to troubled breast;
It drives away the load of sin;
  Gives to the weary rest.

3 Lord, let this balm in wisdom spread
  To earth's remotest bounds,
Till all Thy nations know and speak
  Salvation, joyful sound.

4 The work is Thine, the power is Thine,
  The will Thou hast to give,
Before we feel Thy love divine,
  Thy ransomed powers to save.

NO. 34.

1 TO praise the Lord, a sweet employ,
  Can every Christian sing,
When o'er Thy fullness they survey
  Thy matchless power, O King.

2 Oft does their thoughts in wonder raise,
  When e'er Thy glory shine;
Thy loving kindness and Thy praise,
  Their joy and only theme.

3 Like brothers in one band they stand,
  In love defend the cause,

Maintain the honors of Thy name,
The glory of Thy cross.

4 Lord, strengthen them where e'er they be,
With Thy Almighty power,
That they may flourish as a tree
Surrounded by a tower.

5 The world, the flesh, and Satan, too,
Would hinder if they could,
Opposing them in all they do,
But can't blockade the road.

6 The Lord has promised their support,
And arms them with defense;
Amid the terrors of the road,
In grace they shall advance.

7 But soon their warfare will be o'er,
And all their sorrows end,
A crown of righteousness procure,
And with their Master reign.

8 With Him shall march the golden street
In New Jerusalem;
The song of grace they shall repeat
In worlds that have no end.

NO. 35.

1 CAN I be a soul possessor?
Why so many doubts and fears?
Fear I am but a professor—
None but outward form appears.
Have I got the work within me,
Wrought of God, who reigns above?

Open my eyes, O Lord, and tell me,
　If I'm lead by Thy kind love.

2 If I am, why thus so careless?
　Why not more engaged, I pray—
More engaged in Thy great service?
　Thou who suffered once for me.
Lord decide, the case is pressing;
　Without Thee I cannot live,
And with Thee I have a blessing
　That the world can never give.

3 Tell me, Lord, I pray, O tell me,
　Am I fit a saint to shine?
Teach me how to say, I love Thee,
　And to call Thee ever mine;
Teach my soul the joyful tidings
　That I'm on my journey home;
Soon shall be with Thee abiding,
　Praising Thee upon Thy throne.

NO. 36.

1 JESUS, the author of my faith,
　And the completer too,
For so the Scripture plainly saith,
　And I believe them true.

2 No act of creature can be found,
　But Christ is all in all;
He quickens the poor sinner's mind,
　Lo, with a piercing call.

3 Not with such calls as man can give,
　But reaches in the heart,

And opens out to astonished view
The secrets of His thoughts.

4 I will relate my wretched case
While burdened with my sin,
For long I mourned in misery,
A wretched state was in.

5 Justly condemned I raised my voice
Before Jehovah's throne;
If sent to hell, the sentence just
I must confess and own.

6 Prostrate before the Father's throne
I did my sins confess,
Waiting Thy awful sentence, Lord:
Depart from me ye curs'd!

7 But if Thou can'st, O Lord, be just,
I pray, O let me rest;
Not worthy of honor or trust,
Would seek a servant's place.

8 The Father in compassion moved,
And brought me to the feast:
Thou art my son, fore'er I loved,
Come taste my richest grace.

9 I saw the stream of mercy flow
From Jesus's bleeding side;
My blood, says he, does flow for you,
For you was crucified.

10 Quickly I ran to tell the joy:
That I the Savior seen,
The guilt that did my soul annoy
Was banished with my pain.

11 My neighbors pleased to hear me tell
   What things the Lord had done,
   How that He saved my soul from hell,
   And owned me as a son.

12 My days I will most freely spend
   In his most sweet employ,
   And to His courts I will attend,
   There speak Thy love and joy.

13 Until my days are finished here,
   I will declare Thy name;
   In death I shall have aught to fear,
   Thy glory round me shine.

14 In one vast army shall I see
   Around the dazzling throne,
   Thy loving children in that day,
   In robes of victory shine.

NO. 37. L. M.

1 AH! once I mourned for sin
   That did my spirit grieve;
   Under the burden of my mind
   I prayed, the Lord forgive.

2 My prayers not high did go,
   I smote upon my breast;
   No friendly safeguard could I view
   To save my soul at last.

3 I gave up all for lost,
   And cried with all my breath:
   O, save me, Lord, if can'st be just,
   Or I must sink in death.

4 He heard my plaintive sigh,
    And instantly He sent
  Salvation from his courts on high,
    And cheered me ere I faint.

5 My load of guilt removed,
    And made me feel His power,
  And then I did begin to love,
    Even from that very hour.

6 Pleased with the news, I ran
    To tell how great the joy;
  What a dear Savior I had found,
    To save me ere I die.

7 My friends with me rejoiced,
    For what the Lord had done,
  As many as had heard the voice
    Of God's beloved son.

8 Since then some trials seen,
    Which made me moan and cry,
  But God, who reared me up to man,
    Has cleared my darkest sky.

9 Not far I have advanced
    In my Redeemer's cause;
  The flesh is weak, and foes are strong,
    Which do my way oppose.

10 Keep me in paths divine,
    Low at Thy sacred feet,
  And unto me Thy ear incline,
    Whose mercies are so great.

11 Soon shall the race be run;
    The day is drawing nigh,

The song, on earth only begun,
Shall end above the sky.

NO. 38. L. M.

1 CAN such a worthless worm as I,
    Expect to find in Jesus's name
  A balm to ease my troubled breast,
    And soothe the sorrows of my mind?

2 I sometimes feel I must decline
    And fall away to nothingness;
  O, Lord, uphold me, Thou divine,
    And keep me in Thy righteousness.

3 If, like the wicked, I must prove—
    O! what an unavoiding thought—
  To censure that I do not love
    The Lord, with a kind generous heart.

4 To love Thy people, ways and word,
    I know I feel a strong desire,
  And for their safety on the road
    My heart is oft engaged in prayer.

5 My glimmering hope is faint and small,
    And often makes me doubt and say,
  That if a saint, the least of all
    I must confess, O Lord, to Thee.

6 O, raise my drooping courage up,
    That I may press with vigor on,
  Where doubts and fears will ne'er molest,
    Where tears and sorrows no more come.

7 O, happy day, I soon shall see,
    Whose dawning is my radiant hope,

Where nobler songs I'll sing to Thee,
Who is my only safe resort.

NO. 39. S. M.

1 O, TEACH me what I am,
   Thou maker of my frame,
For Thou dost know what is in man,
   From whence his spirit came.

2 Vileness corrupts me here,
   And anguish fills my mind,
In dread before my God appear,
   The just and Holy One.

3 I know that Thou art good;
   Just in all Thy ways,
Thou hast command of my abode
   In everlasting days.

4 Teach me the way of peace,
   And fit my soul to shine,
To trust in Redeemer's grace;
   Call Thee forever mine.

5 No other way I know
   Can e'er ascend to Thee;
But where Thy truth and mercy glow,
   Our safe retreat on high.

6 The road our Saviour went,
   His daily walk foretell,
Salvation through His name is sent
   To souls deserving hell.

NO. 40.   S. M.

1 THE Lord, my strength and hope,
   My everlasting all,
 My comfort even to cheer me up
   When in afflictions fall.

2 He is my hiding place,
   When storms of sorrow rise ;
 Defend my soul against such vice
   As vanity and lies.

3 My portion and my all
   In Thee I freely trust ;
 Thou dost Thy pleasure and Thy will,
   And still does what is just.

4 At Thy command I stand ;
   At Thy command I go ;
 At Thy command I'll close this scene,
   And leave this below.

5 Thy pleasure may I gain,
   And find acceptance there,
 To view the New Jerusalem,
   And of her glories share.

NO. 41.—145TH PSALM.—C. M.

1 The Lord has mercy and is good
   To every living thing
 That walks upon this earthly clod ;
   Their bounty from him spring.

2 All things by him was form'd and made,
   And yet unknown to man,

THE WANDERING PILGRIM.

The glory that He has prepared
Within the secret plan.

3 'Tis from His bounteous giving hand
Our wants are all supplied,
And nigh to all that call on Him
In truth they shall abide.

4 The wicked can't before Him stand
In that great judgment day;
He will reward each at their hand,
The deeds they love to obey.

NO. 42.   S. M.

1 O, COME away my thoughts,
And leave the world alone;
Remember nature is but dross,
And soon must be consumed.

2 Then I must soar away
To worlds that are unknown,
To the bright world of endless day,
Or sink beneath a frown.

3 Think on thy future state—
What 'tis to wear a crown,
And at thy Saviour's table eat.
And praise Him on the throne.

4 The Church to Him ascribe
Her honor and her praise;
In Him her members shall abide
In everlasting days.

5 The wicked shall go way
In chains reserved for them,

And there in endless ages stay
In worlds that have no end.

NO. 43. P. M.

1 THERE'S many ways proposed
　To flee the wrath of God,
But all the Scriptures prove
　There's but one heavenly road.
Straight through the world this road does go,
None but believers e'er can know.

2 The Lord will lead along
　The followers of the Lamb,
And with a mighty arm
　Shall bring them conqueror's home.
And all their songs from first to last
Will be the song of grace, free grace.

3 Not works that we have done,
　E'er brought us in the way,
But Thy good pleasure won
　Our souls from misery;
Else we had still gone on in sin,
And misery would our portion been.

4 Unto the Lord declare,
　To Him our praise be given,
Whilst we His mercies share
　Till we arrive in heaven;
There reign in one perpetual day
With Christ to all eternity.

NO. 44. S. M.

BAPTISM.

1 ARISE and be baptised,
   Ye living children come,
Obedience to your Lord, apprised
   By every heaven born son.

2 The pattern here He gave,
   That we should follow in,
To fall beneath the yielding wave
   And rise quite clear from sin.

3 It does the conscience clear
   Though humbling to the flesh,
While faith and hope new courage bear
   And clothes the soul afresh.

4 This robe we here put on,
   In our profession make,
Our faith implanted in the Son
   Who never will forsake.

5 This robe unspotted be
   Let heaven's heirs adorn,
Much happiness we hear shall see
   In keeping thy command.

6 And when our race is run
   And we from time remove,
A nobler robe we shall put on
   Adorned with grace and love.

NO. 45.   L. M.

1 ON Jordan's banks the Baptist stood
Immersing there beneath the flood,
Jesus Himself the pattern gave
Bending beneath the rising wave.

2 Repenting souls the pattern take,
All other ways and means forsake;
Follow your Lord, lo, all things well,
All other ways leads down to hell.

3 Though many ways are now proposed
To save expense or health expose;
Religionist of the present day
These schemes are laid to lead away.

4 But the Almighty God did know,
And laid the plan for us to go;
And in obeying his precepts
There is a great reward annexed.

5 He's made it plain and sure and straight
And leading into Zion's gate,
And children of the heavenly King
While on their journey sweetly sing.

NO. 46.   P. M.

1 BAPTISM is a sacred right
  Unto believers here,
Enjoined on sons of God's delight
Fleeing from Egypt's darkest night
  And to his courts appear.

2 The church will hear with solemn awe,
  Their zeal for happiness,

THE WANDERING PILGRIM.

What they had sought out by the law
And failed therein to find out how,
  To ease up their distress.

3 But meeting Jesus by the way,
    Who said, come follow me,
  I can release your bonded chains,
  Give ease to all your troubled pains,
    I am the only way.

3 But self and nature must deny,
    Follow the pattern gave,
  Take up your cross the shame despised
  And like your Master be baptised
    Beneath the yielding wave.

4 With joy we will to Zion go
    Since Jesus deems to save,
  There seek to follow Jesus through,
  The great example, there to do,
    Beneath the yielding wave.

5 Yea, Zion's children will say, come!
    Who knows his power to save;
  Extended hands say here is room
  Welcome the exile to his home,
    Anew in life to live.

6 These duties here enjoined on us
    Esteemed no easy task,
  But soon relieves a troubled mind
  And send new joy from heaven divine,
    More than one dare to ask.

7 But soon these joys and sorrows here
    Must yield unto the grave,
  There happy shall our thoughts appear

When Jesus shall again draw near,
We'll sing his power to save.

NO. 47.   S. M

1 BENEATH the gentle wave
  He laid his sacred head,
An emblem of his power to save
  Poor sinners from the dead.

2 Thus did our Lord portray
  His wisdom here below,
Recorded then for us to obey
  Who loves his precepts too.

3 We will the sample show,
  Now by the water's side,
There converts claim they love him too
  His name is all their pride.

4 May solemn reverence bow
  O'er the poor sinner's round,
While these young converts go to show
  They have the Saviour found.

5 They bow their heads beneath
  The rolling waters poured,
·Arise anew to live by faith
  Upon the Son of God.

* * *· * * *

6 The work is done, and yet
  There's time and room for more;
Come, humble sinner, here is meat
  Your Saviour to adore.

7 Why will you now delay
  Your burdened cross to bear,

We will assist you here to-day,
O, come, and never fear.

8 If you for goodness wait
You'll never come at all;
In wating for a larger hope
The one you have will fall.

9 Until it is so weak
You'll claim it none at all,
And drag along 'twixt fear and hope
To live alone withal.

NO. 48.

1 I SHOULD the waters tread,
If sure I was aware
In God's fair book of life could read
My name was e'en written there.

2 Duty would be no task
O could I now decide,
Jehovah would upon me bask
In smiles of love and pride.

3 O Lord decide my case,
With hope and love and fear,
I will my duty now embrace
E'er in thy courts appear.

4 With faith and love and zeal,
May I in duty shine,
And with my brethren know and feel
The effects of love divine.

NO. 49.   P. M.

1 O MAY these gentle waters
   Now in compassion flow,
While Zion's sons and daughters
   Beneath her waves do go;
Their Master did the example lay
And calls on them now to obey;
With willing steps they move,
Their hope and calling prove.

2 The sinners round are gazing
   In scorn of wild dismay,
Whilst others look amazing
   And choose some other way;
But willing subjects will approve
And follow him they truly love,
Though wicked men deride
They'll choose the flowing tide.

3 Though to the flesh 'tis humbling
   To fall beneath the wave,
And oft we hear much grumbling
   About this watery grave.
The flesh is weak, our fears prolong—
Our hope confirm while faith is strong
For oft we see delay
Put off, not to obey.

4 O Lord give converts, pastor,
   Both grace and strength to stand,
Obeying their protector
   Requires a self-command;
All things in order duty shine,
And looks both heavenly and divine

In tokens of that day
When we shall rise with Thee.

NO. 50.   C. M.

FELLOWSHIP.

1 HOW would my heart rejoice to hear
   My brother welcome say,
In Zion let us now appear,
   And keep a solemn day.

2 Then with the heart emblazoned up
   With love and truth and zeal,
Would with a brighter courage look,
   Anew our hopes would feel.

3 Dear Lord, O haste the day indeed,
   When sin and grief and shame,
In banishment of thought or word,
   Will ne'er our hearts profane.

4 'Twould be a heaven here below
   To feel quite clear from sin;
None but our blest Redeemer know,
   And on His name recline.

5 But 'tis our lot, should ne'er repine
   At what our God thinks best;
And if we fall may we recline
   And on His bosom rest.

6 We know this earthly house must fall,
   Its walls are giving in,
Then heaven to our souls withal
   Her glories will be seen.

NO. 51. C. M.

1 O, BLESS the Lord, my soul rejoice,
   And praise the Saviour's name,
Lift up, ye saints, the heavenly voice,
   The dead revives again.

2 Jesus, the Son of God, appears,
   In majesty and power,
While on His brow a glimmer bears
   These lively hopes of ours.

3 His name revives our courage up
   To battle for the right,
And while I live be this my hope,
   He will my steps direct.

4 He's promised my supporter be,
   Through all my journey here,
And when the creature help all flee,
   In death I need not fear.

5 Dear Lord, my soul I pray to bless,
   That while I live below,
May set Thee forth my righteousness,
   And nothing else to know.

6 And when my course is finished here,
   Welcome may I receive,
Joyful to part with care and fear,
   And rise anew to live.

NO. 52. C. M.

1 COME, friends, and tell if e'er you felt
   The pardoning of God,
Applied to cleanse your souls from guilt,
   By the Redeemer's blood.

THE WANDERING PILGRIM.   51

2 Come, tell how that your joys arise,
   What sorrows you sustain,
  How grace decays and comfort dies,
   And leaves the heart in pain.

3 Tell what reviving seasons seen,
   Since first you knew the Lord,
  Tell how your hope is centered in
   The Saviour and His word.

4 From pains and joys we get along,
   While dwelling here below,
  Adhere to Christ, the living song,
   To aid our journey through.

5 He tells us that we must expect
   Much conflicts here below,
  But soon these trials we'll outride,
   And all our sorrows too.

6 Where pain and death is feared no more,
   Our souls must shortly fly,
  With joy and grace we shall adore
   The God that rules the sky.

7 These joys and pains with doubts and fears,
   Soon in exchange be given,
  For nobler joys in endless years,
   With all the host of heaven.

NO. 53.   S. M.

1 COME while your hearts are warm,
   Inflamed with love and zeal,
  Attend the Zion of our God,
   Through every woe or weal.

2 Your aid will help support
   This earthly temple here,
While loving brethren will report
   Your name in love and fear.

3 Zion, whose doors are great,
   Stands open night and day,
And all her loving children greet
   Her precepts to obey.

NO. 54.   C. M.

1 Once in my time I started out
   In wisdom's paths to tread;
I had a generous noble friend,
   It was my Brother and I.

CHORUS.
It was a bright and summer day,
   The forest was quite green;
Our hearts were light, it was the May
   By every Christian seen.

2 We walked apace with ease and speed,
   Each other pleased to try
To catch a glimpse of joy o'erspread,
   It was my Brother and I.

CHORUS.
It was a bright and summer day,
   The forest was quite green;
Our hearts were light, it was the May
   By every Christian seen.

3 And as we neared, Autumn appeared,
   The leaves began to dry,

But still our hearts the path revered,
It was my Brother and I.

CHORUS.

There was some Autumn clouds withal
O'er us, with the sunshine;
The sunshine and the clouds of Fall
By every Christian seen.

4 Ah, soon Winter to us appeared,
Our path was frozen nigh,
Our hearts grew cold, no more revered,
To say, my Brother and I.

CHORUS.

The winter winds and snows were high,
They covered up the green;
These wintry seasons did us try,
By every Christian seen.

5 Our way ice-bound we could not chide;
New paths we chose to try;
Our separation was too wide
To say, my Brother and I.

CHORUS.

The wintry winds and snows were high,
They covered up the green;
These wintry seasons did us try,
By every Christian seen.

6 The path I roved it verily proved
To lead me off to die;
My steps retraced, backwards I moved
To find my Brother and I.

CHORUS.

The winter's past, the snows were off,
The fields looked bright and green,

These changing seasons very oft
By every Christian seen.

7 We met, and O, what joy to find
The winter was passed by;
O, fault was passioned by the wind,
It was my Brother and I.

CHORUS.

The winter's past, the snows were off,
The fields looked bright and green,
These changing seasons very oft
By every Christian seen.

8 Since then I've learned to look beyond
The blue ethereal sky;
Love covers up, lo, many faults,
Between my Brother and I.

CHORUS.

The winter's past, the snows were off,
The fields looked bright and green,
These changing seasons very oft
By every Christian seen.

9 O, man of God, look up and see
What dangerous foes will try
To cause a separation here,
Between thy Brother and I.

CHORUS.

It is the hope, the blissful peace,
To every Christian given;
Ere soon sorrows will release
For better days in heaven.

NO. 55.   C. M.

1 BRETHREN, let love now be your aim,
   In singleness of heart;
God's love does cover in the man
   A multitude of fault.

2 Without this love our faults will fall,
   Our Brothers will arise;
Shortsightedness we can't see all,
   Far off they reach the skies.

3 When love is cold, our eyes eclipsed,
   It looks quite dark within,
While through the beams of nature's rays
   Small moats are always seen.

4 But love to God and love to man
   Gives us a precious store;
Without this love 'twould be in vain
   To knock at mercy's door.

5 Dear Lord, inspire my soul with love,
   To feel a brother's care,
While all my thoughts are raised above
   His imperfections here.

NO. 56.   S. M.

PARTING HYMN.

1 OUR meeting here has been
   Of one harmonious theme,
While love and friendship well unites
   Our songs in Christ, our King.

2 Our parting now must come,
   Awhile at least must go;

Our cares on earth must be adorned
For good while here below.

3 A parting hand oft makes
    The penitential tear
To flow in torrents down the cheeks
    Of God's dear children here.

4 The time must shortly come,
    To cares we'll bid adieu,
And with a parting hand we'll say,
    Farewell, my sorrows too.

5 Farewell, my friends, awhile,
    In bonds of Christian love,
We trust kind Providence will smile,
    We all shall meet above.

6 We all shall meet above,
    Who for the Saviour look,
His care is over those in love,
    And all their sorrows took.

NO. 57.   S. M.

ELECTION AND PRESERVATION.

1 THIS earthly house must fall,
    We have a building high,
Prepared by God and safe for all
    The chosen family.

2 I pray, Dear Lord, embrace
    My never-dying soul;
O, may I feel electing grace,
    'Tis Thee can make me whole.

THE WANDERING PILGRIM. 57

3 O, fit me for Thy praise,
  That when I'm called to die,
Without a vail in endless days,
  Praise Thee who bled for me.

NO. 58. C. M.

1 THE children of the kingdom here
    In outer darkness driven,
  While children of the Gentile race
    Shall now possess their heaven.

2 The Jews were blessed in many a way
    Above their fellows here,
  But Jesus calls the Gentile race,
    Within His courts appear.

3 The Jews, with stubborn heart and will,
    Would not their Saviour own,
  Because His parentage befel
    Below an earthly throne.

4 The Gentiles of the Jewish race
    Shall truth and wisdom see,
  While Jews with all their stores of grace
    Shall still rejected be.

5 The halt, the lame, the blind were called
    Unto the wedding feast,
  While men of quite pretended fame
    Disdained to be a guest.

6 We see a difference still is made,
    While men of low degree
  Are called to own their Saviour, God,
    And willing subjects be.

7 While seldom men of high renown
    Are called by sovereign grace,
  Take up their cross, despise the shame,
    Their natural will debase.

NO. 59.   P. M.

1 PRAISES to our Intercessor
    For His love and wondrous plan,
  Coming as a mediator,
    Saving lost and ruined man.
  As God's only Son he came here,
    From His shining courts on high,
  Opened a way for the poor sinner,
    Through His name should never die.

2 God did view our situation
    In sending His only Son,
  Laid a plan of free salvation
    To redeem His favorite one.
  O, such love as this was shown us,
    Can poor mortals e'er declare,
  Jesus in His pity owned us,
    Raised us up from keen despair.

3 He now says, ye are my chosen,
    Saved by grace from first to last,
  And in gathering I will lose none,
    In my hands I'll hold you fast.
  O, what a strong deliverer
    Sinners now have got to praise;
  Be ye strong in faith, believer,
    In His praise spend all your days.

NO. 60.   L. M.

1 O, WHAT a worthless worm am I,
   Born of the dust and vanity;
   I'm filled with sin and misery too,
   And deep in debt and ought to pay.

2 Nothing within myself can do,
   That will release the vengeance due;
   So says the law, a wise decree,
   The soul that sins shall surely die.

3 Jesus, my intercessor, freed
   And paid the debt the law decreed,
   By standing in my room to die,
   The law of God to justify.

4 He took away my heart of steel,
   And gave a heart to know and feel,
   A glimpse to see a wretched case,
   Without my sins they were erased.

5 Now to the law I quickly flew,
   To know what this poor soul must do;
   But I soon found no entrance there;
   My soul gave up in keen despair.

6 Mercy was now my only plea,
   Thy mercy grant or I must die;
   I'm well aware if sent to hell,
   Thy righteous law approves it well.

7 But Thou, dear Jesus, all the while,
   Did see me in my greatest toil,
   Proclaimed to me, I am the way,
   Leave off thy sins and follow me.

8 At once I saw the way was plain,
Through Christ, believers, they must come,
And Thee, dear Jesus, once despised,
Did now receive my warmest praise.

9 His banner o'er my soul was love,
While feasting me on things above;
I felt His grace so rich and free,
To save a sinner lost like me.

NO. 61.   C. M.

1 WHY was I made to hear Thy voice,
   The Lord of righteousness,
Whilst many souls take misery's choice,
   And scan the work of grace.

2 Why was I made to feel my sins?
   A load that brought me low,
And all my crimes, my sinful crimes,
   The Lord did to me show.

3 Why was I made to love His name,
   And speak His joys abroad?
Whilst thousands better than I am
   Still choose the road that's wide.

4 It is the Lord, 'tis his free grace,
   That opened mine eyes to see;
It is the Lord that speaks peace, peace,
   And says, lovest thou me?

5 Else I had still refused to hear
   The councils of a friend,
And in my wickedness appear
   As chaff before the wind.

6 Thanks be unto the Lord, our God,
   For blessings of the feast,
 Revealed to me, His holy word
   Approved, a welcome guest.

NO. 62.   C. M.

1 IN Zion, city of our God,
   Is there the tree of life,
 There is the tree whose fruit afford
   Our great immortal strife.

2 Its leaves are good to cleanse the stain
   In which our soul's immersed,
 To cure the leper, heal the lame,
   And lead our minds to Christ.

3 The Revelator saw this tree,
   In visions on the Isle;
 Happy the man such visions see,
   Condensed in love and zeal.

4 No less than Christ this tree can be,
   Here's food for dying souls;
 His blood upon Mount Calvary
   Was shed to make them whole.

5 To cleanse the stain which sin has made,
   And purge the vital part,
 Renew the spirit of the mind,
   And give a contrite heart.

6 A heart believing true and clean,
   That feels a Saviour near,
 A heart despising every sin
   That rage in envy here.

7 Great God, O may I taste this fruit,
   And prove its healing power;
   I feel a need to cleanse my guilt,
   Almost in every hour.

NO. 63.   C. M.

1 THERE is much said of late, about
   Our poor old Baptist friends;
   Many vile stories have gone out
   That does much mischief lend.

2 Some of my neighbors plainly tell,
   Can't bear to hear them preach;
   Their damning doctrine came from hell,
   And heaven it cannot reach.

3 No doubt it cuts their stony hearts,
   Some like in days of old;
   When Jesus preached in different parts,
   The Pharisees he told.

4 Ye compass sea and land as well,
   To make one proselyte;
   When made, he is the child of hell,
   Two fold more than your weight.

5 And in this present day we're told,
   Deceivers should arise,
   In saint's array they stand up bold,
   As wolves when in disguise.

6 And from the Holy Writ we're informed
   That some should be deceived,
   Some that have not of God been born,
   Nor tasted of His love.

7 But the dear soul that's born of God,
　　His name's forever sealed,
　E'er in the great atonement made,
　　By Jesus 'tis revealed.

8 Our God is love, and we love Him,
　　Because he first loved us;
　He opened the way, and in due time
　　Brought us to taste His grace.

9 He bringeth all His little lambs,
　　To them an unsought way,
　Redeeming them from death and bonds,
　　By Christ upon the tree.

10 They are a poor despised race,
　　By mortals here below,
　But God, in whom they put their trust,
　　Has conquered every foe.

11 Both death and hell, at His command,
　　Must yield up all their prey,
　And saints will join the heavenly band
　　At the great rising day.

12 They'll bid farewell to every foe,
　　Through Jesus's name proclaim
　Their Saviour and deliverer too,
　　When all their foes are slain.

NO. 64.

1 A MIGHTY foe within the breast
　　Of every Christian lay,
　At war with God, a mighty pest,
　He will their every hope molest—
　　Who can this rival be?

2 He is no less an earthly mind,
    Displaying worldly power,
  Contentious, and of most unkind,
  Together with the world combined,
    Conceives a cross to bear.

3 Were not his subjects to their King,
    Submissive when he spake,
  Would soon destroy the tidy wing
  That brings the music which they sing,
    From heaven's loftiest peak.

4 But grace and wisdom o'er him shine,
    Set forth a portly man;
  He looks quite humble and divine,
  We would suppose a willing mind,
    Only while wisdom reign.

5 Ere long they'll drop this envious man,
    The grave must be his doom,
  The spirit 'turned from whence it came,
  Where nobler joys will be entwined
    In heaven, the Christian's home.

6 But in the resurection morn
    The graves assunder spread,
  Mortality, be clothed divine,
  United with the great to shine
    In Christ their living head.

NO. 65.   S. M.

1 I'LL praise my God to-day,
    For all His favors shown,
  He gives my order to obey,
    And make His mercies known.

THE WANDERING PILGRIM.

2 To tell to sinners round
    The mercies of my God;
What a dear Saviour I have found,
    What joy the word afford.

3 He left the courts on high,
    And came here to redeem,
While wicked hands did crucify
    What God before ordained.

4 He did behold my state,
    While hanging on the tree,
And O, how miserable fate,
    If he'd not pitied me.

5 He took away my guilt
    And pardoned all my sin,
Yea, freely justified in sight
    Of God, my Father, King.

6 And in due time He called :
    Poor sinner follow me;
Without a murmur left off all,
    Behold my heart and see.

7 Some precious seasons seen,
    Since first I knew the Lord,
While dark and dreary nights have spread
    Their shadows round my head.

8 How long His favor lend,
    The Lord does only know;
He is my great preserving friend,
    While dwelling here below.

NO. 66.   C. M.

1 LET wolves and lions howl around,
    Where all my children dwell,
  They 'pear to shake the solid ground,
    The very gates of hell.

2 Fear not, ye little chosen band,
    A remnant weak and small;
  'Tis I that holds you in my hand,
    They cannot harm your soul.

3 'Tis I that guards your daily road,
    That leads to Zion's hill,
  'Tis I your daily comforts spread
    Around the place you dwell.

4 Ah, soon you'll gain those heavenly heights
    On the fair banks above;
  Behold your Saviour face to face,
    In flowing streams of love.

5 There drink at the great fountain spring,
    Where love like waters flow,
  Where anxious cares will cease to sting,
    To sorrows bid adieu.

NO. 67.   C. M.

1 IN that bright world so far away,
    The Christians all will join,
  To praise the Lord in that Great Day,
    In heaven their glorious home.

2 Though troubles interfere and mar,
    And make discord while here,

THE WANDERING PILGRIM. 67

Soon shall they go where is no jar,
Nothing to wish or fear.

3 As shining lights around the throne,
    Shall every Christian be
In heaven, their everlasting home,
    To all eternity.

NO. 68.   L. M.

JUDGMENT DAY.

1 LET sinners watch and groan and pray,
In dread to see the Eternal Day,
While saints delight to sing the theme,
Dear Jesus, come, O quickly come!

2 The spirited and mighty men,
In guilt and folly must look down,
Afraid to appear before that God
So wise, so great, so just and good.

3 Their souls repentance never knew,
To whom God's vengeance now is due,
Down to eternity must go,
With all the wrath of God to know.

4 O, saints of every age rejoice,
Your souls shall hear God's milder voice;
With Him ere long you soon shall be,
And spend one everlasting day.

5 In that bright world of endless bliss,
Where each shall wear a smiling face,
There sing that new, that living song,
Without a lisp or stammering tongue.

NO. 69.

1 DEATH, like an overflowing stream,
    Sweeps life from us away,
And leaves this body, mortal frame,
    For nature to decay.

2 The time appointed of our God
    Comes flying swiftly on,
Conveys us to our last abode,
    To worlds that are unknown.

3 Great God, O teach our souls the way
    Prepared and fit to rise,
That when Thy summons bids us fly,
    Shall sing Thy nobler praise.

4 In hopes of that Eternal Day,
    Our souls do humbly wait,
Yea, praying in this mortal clay
    For entrance at Thy gate.

NO. 70. C. M.

1 HOW can I bear the word, depart!
    In that Great Judgment Day;
Dear Lord, if I do love Thee not,
    I pray awaken me.

2 Give me a heart to know and feel
    My sins are all forgiven,
A full redemption Thou hast sealed
    Within Thy courts in heaven.

3 I know I shall be satisfied
    When I awake with Thee;
With Thee, my Lord, my living head,
    In likeness shall I be.

NO. 71.

DEATH.

1 DEATH is a monster many fear,
Though soon or late he will appear;
With certainty he strikes the blow,
All earthly means cannot withdraw.

2 The solemn thought, how sad thou art,
When changing seasons called to part;
To bid adieu to all below,
And rise with Christ or sink in woe.

3 Happy the saint when he appears,
Unseals the great dividing bars
That frees his soul from sorrow here,
And rise to endless pleasures there.

4 A crown of love is there prepared,
That Jesus will place on his head,
A robe of righteousness supply,
And with Him reign eternally.

5 Often I view their happy lot,
And wish I were among the flock;
For all I can but wish and pray,
And long to see that glorious day.

NO. 72.   C. M.

1 O, YOUTH, the spark of life's gone down,
   Thy days are numbered here,
Thy body to the dust return,
   To moulder and decay.

2 Thy soul return to God who gave;
   He calls and thou must go;

Soon must we e'er all follow thee,
And leave this world below.

3 Be this our happiness below,
That when we're called to die,
We leave an evidence to show
Our home's in heaven on high.

NO. 73. L. M.

[Written upon the death of Elder Benjamin Martin,
December 9, 1852.]

1 OUR under shepherd, husband, friend,
From time to eternity has gone;
Triumphantly he reigns above,
And views a smiling God in love.

2 For many years he labored here,
And preached the word to many an ear;
His labors blessed with reverenced fear,
To needy sinners far and near.

3 The churches here esteemed him dear,
When in their presence did appear;
In absence they did long to see
The time for him with them to be.

4 But now he's gone to his long home,
From whence no traveler return;
With Jesus there he'll wear a crown,
Where storms of sorrow never come.

5 Far better to depart and be,
Our loss his gain eternally,
Where in a nobler, sweeter strain,
He'll sing that new, that living song.

[The same.]
NO. 74. C. M.

1 O, THOU art gone, whom we esteemed,
   A father, brother, friend;
   Thy flesh lies silent in the tomb,
   Thy soul above the sky.

2 Trials caressed thy nature here,
   With sore afflictions too;
   But God, in whom thou loved to serve,
   Upheld thee, e'en till now.

3 A faithful soldier proved to be,
   While watching o'er the flock
   That God our Saviour planted here,
   And called him forth to guard.

4 We must still mourn that thou art gone,
   For all 'tis well with thee;
   Happy did'st die in God's dear Son,
   Now dwells with Him on high.

5 He does now use a golden harp,
   With strings forever new;
   A harp to sing that God is love,
   All-wise and perfect too.

6 How soon shall we join in the song,
   There sing unceasing praise,
   To God, the Lamb, with heavenly tongues,
   In everlasting days.

NO. 75. C. M.

1 THE dying saint is heard to say,
   Dear Jesus quickly come,
   And waft this soul of mine away,
   To its eternal home.

2 Afflictions, cares, and toils and pain,
    Has numbered here my days,
  While some most precious seasons seen
    In my Redeemer's praise.

3 Farewell, dear wife, and children too,
    I leave you in God's care;
  No more expect to trouble you
    With sore afflictions here.

4 Walk in the path that's sure and straight,
    Which leads to joys on high,
  Think on death's cold and gloomy fate,
    Without the Saviour's love.

5 We ne'er can reign with Christ above,
    Without a change of heart;
  O, may the Lord teach you to love
    And choose the wiser part.

6 His glorious presence overshades
    And hides the monster, death;
  Nothing to fear with such an aid,
    But pant away my breath.

7 I know that He will soon arrive,
    And willingly I go;
  In Jesus's arms I fall asleep,
    Soft as downy pillows are.

8 O, what a blood-washed throng I'll meet,
    And reign with them above;
  To march the heavenly golden street,
    And sing undying love.

NO. 76.   L. M.

1 HOW short the race our friend has run,
   As yesterday his days begun;
   Time's fleeting scythe has cut him down,
   The morning sun goes down at noon.

2 The old, the young in sympathy
   Should on this think, I too must die;
   But yet we run quite heedless on,
   Nor take one thought till death has won.

3 Great God, awake the stupid mind,
   That from this lesson he may find,
   'Tis but to leave the world alone,
   And meditate what soon must come.

4 And sinners too, I deeply feel,
   Could you but see your course, bewail,
   But you are blind to all that's good,
   And none can open you eyes but God.

5 I pray, O God, Thy will be done,
   If 'tis Thy pleasure, Thou canst bring,
   Thy awful truth their minds impress,
   To come to Thee, our righteousness.

6 Be near with those whose lot has fell
   To bid a friend the last farewell,
   Thy presence might e'er reign with them,
   And teach them lessons in Thy name.

7 Thy love shall crown the work at last,
   With all thy chosen ransom race;
   Grace, Grace, shall be their happy song,
   And Heaven their everlasting home.

NO. 77.   C. M.

[Composed on the last sickness of a young friend.]

1 TO thee, my friend, it does appear,
 Death stares your lovely face;
 I pray, O God be with thee here,
 To bless with love and peace.

2 How can I bear to see thee go
 While in thy youthful days,
 But we must part while here below,
 For so the Word declares.

3 Have you a hope that is steadfast,
 Anchored within the veil,
 A hope that Jesus has embraced
 Your name in worlds above.

4 A hope that Jesus is your friend,
 Who'll be forever nigh,
 And in that last great trying hour,
 Will bring thee home on high.

5 A hope that Jesus once did die,
 Poor rebels to redeem;
 Salvation sent from God on high,
 Through his beloved Son.

6 A hope that you may see that place,
 Where all will be complete,
 And see your Saviour face to face,
 There walk the golden street.

NO. 78.   C. M.

1 DEATH like an Indian arrow flies,
  And hastens us away,
  Prepared or unprepared, he cries,
  Thou canst no longer stay.

2 Stung with the jaws of death and sin,
  My spirit waiting stands,
  Till God shall bid my soul arise,
  I'll go when He commands.

3 No earthly theme will court my stay,
  Her joys have poisoned me,
  Blasted my hope and laid me low,
  In dust and vanity.

4 But God did view my drooping head,
  And sent Salvation nigh,
  Aroused my fears, revived the dead
  For better joys on high.

NO. 79.   P. M.

[Written by request of Deacon McLeod, upon the death of his wife.]

1 O, HOW blest the sister bereft,
  Afflictions are all left behind,
  Not like the husband she's left,
  Must grovel with nature his time.
  She gave her friends an evidence,
  Prepared to see her Saviour and Prince,
  And longed to see that happy place,
  And dwell with him in love and peace.

HER CHARGE.

2 I charge thee, my daughter and son,
   Thy father remember with care,
The Lord, thy rewarder when done,
   If thou'll remember my prayer.
Afflicted and old, his days are most o'er,
   From suffering must have kind care,
This must be expected from you,
   I pray thou, remember my prayer.

3 The counsel of a mother take,
   See to thy heart what's treasured there,
   I pray thou remember my prayer.
O, would the Lord awaken your mind,
   And teach you to love and to fear,
I then could leave you freely behind,
   Hoping that you would meet me there.

4 Farewell husband, daughter and son,
   The Lord calls and freely I obey,
Gladly to leave all under the sun,
   With Jesus forever to be.
Farewell friends, one and all,
In Jesus' arms how sweetly I fall,
   And die triumphantly a saint.

NO. 80.   P. M.

[Written at the tomb of Eld. Benj. Martin.]

1 I'VE come to the place
   Where the aged pilgrim lies,
In silence to view
The grave, Where is he?
His feelings at rest,
And his soul borne away

THE WANDERING PILGRIM. 77

In triumph with Jesus
Forever to be.

2 Ineffable joys
His table surround,
With pleasures of peace,
And a Sabbath of rest,
Where troubles will cease
His spirit to wound,
And cares and afflictions
No more can oppress.

3 Through valleys, o'er hills,
And mountains rough ways,
His footsteps have traced
And marked their way through ;
As a servant of God,
He was chosen to preach
A glorious salvation
To Adam's lost race.

4 He warned them of misery,
In dying in sin,
And expounded to them
The lost state they were in.
By sin and transgression,
Rebelled against God,
And at the great judgment
Should reap their reward.

5 Now brethren and sisters,
Do mourn that he's gone,
Though his gain, yet we feel
'Tis the loss we sustain ;
As a pastor, a leader,
A father and friend,

He gave the example
Our motives should tend.

6 Though imperfect in part,
Now that part's done away,
Outrode all his conflicts,
Through Death's dark valley,
No doubt long ere now
He has joined that band,
That marches the coast
Of Emanuel's land.

NO. 81.   P. M.
HEAVEN.

1 O HAPPY place where Jesus reigns,
   'Tis far above the sky,
A place I sometimes hope to see,
But fear again 'tis not for me,
   Where pleasures never die.

2 A place where Jesus deigns to bless
   The people of his choice;
A place where foes no more molest,
No more to feel the sin oppress,
   That hides a smiling face.

3 O, happy place, I still must say,
   I long to reach that shore,
My soul has had a sweet foretaste,
Where storms are o'er and winter's past,
   And O, I sigh for more.

4 That name makes glad the dying saint
   Who sings his sins forgiven;
In Jesus' arms he wants to faint—
No more to mourn his sorrows quaint,
   But rise to joys in heaven.

NO. 82.   S. M.

1 What strong cementing ties
 Unites the Christian love
 Within the hidden bosom lies
 A taste of joys above.

2 How strong when called to part
 For seasons here below—
 They stand united, hand and heart,
 In joys the world can't know.

3 Give me a place, O Lord,
 Within Thy humble court,
 Tasting the fruits Thy grace afford,
 My heart to them unite.

4 May Christian love unite
 Thy children here below,
 Thy name should be their whole delight,
 No other name to know.

NO. 83.   L. M.

1 THE Lord is called the sinner's friend,
 Through him our hopes of heaven depend,
 He calls by sovereign grace applied,
 And points to Jesus' bleeding side.

2 The sinner hears the heavenly voice,
 Yea, then prepares to make his choice,
 While God at once the rule applied,
 And points to Jesus' bleeding side.

3 The soul condemned to death's dark shade,
 Awaken'd by the Holy Word,
 Can point to Jesus' bleeding side,
 And say, behold the way to God.

4 He is the way the Prophets taught,
That God's dear people should be brought;
By faith look forward to that day,
When the Messiah they should see.

5 They died without a living sight;
By faith their acceptance was all right.
Ah, blessed eyes for them that saw,
Thrice blessed they by faith do know.

5 O God, now condescend to be
A friend to poor unworthy me;
May I by faith apply the Word,
And say, behold the way to God.

NO. 84. S. M.

1 THERE is a heaven above,
    A God to glorify;
  O, may my tongue with grace and love,
    This truth to verify.

2 But self must be denied,
    Or he will break our peace;
  Confirmed by foes on every side,
    Much wisdom ne'er possess.

3 The Lord, by Sovereign grace,
    His subjects freely call,
  Implants within their minds afresh,
    A hope of humble zeal.

4 He took our fathers' hand,
    To lead in their distress,
  Sojourning through that barren land,
    Unto the land of rest.

5 But now our pity pleads,
   Through his beloved Son;
   Renew the heart, supply our needs,
   And lead by grace divine.

6 His promises confirmed,
   A better hope is given,
   Our trials here will be exchanged
   For nobler days in heaven.

NO. 85.   P. M.

1 I'M on my journey home,
   To meet my God and friend,
   Where congregations ne'er break up,
   And Sabbaths never end.

CHORUS.

O, who will go with me,
O, who will go with me,
Where congregations ne'er break up,
And Sabbaths never end.

2 My heart rejoic'd to meet
   My Saviour and my God—
   Meet him who cancelled all my debt,
   Ten thousand talents owed

[Chorus.]   O, who will go with me, &c.

3 Poor sinners covered o'er
   With sin, and shame and fear,
   Could you but see the grief he bore
   Upon Mount Calvary.

[Chorus.]   O, who will go with me, &c.

4 How would your hearts rejoice,
   To know He died for thee,
 While looking heavenward, exclaim,
   Thy grace sufficient be.
[Chorus.]   O, who will go with me, &c.

5 But soon the time will come,
   The journey's end I view;
 I'll see without a veil between
   The God that bled for me.

CHORUS.
O, who will go with me,
O, who will go with me,
Where congregations ne'er break up;
And Sabbaths never end.

NO. 86.   C. M.

1 O, MAY Thy children, O our God,
   In Zion's court appear,
 There spread their wants before Thy face,
   And worship in Thy fear.

2 In solemn awe their wants express,
   Before their Father's throne,
 Trusting in Thy sufficient grace,
   Through Thy beloved Son.

3 O, may they trust in Thee alone
   For wisdom, faith and zeal,
 And look beyond the watchman here,
   For strength in every ill.

4 O, may their peace spread far and wide,
   A boon to sinners round,
 Rejoicing in Thy hand to guide
   Them to Emanuel's ground.

NO. 87.   C. M.

MORNING DEVOTION.

1 THE rising sun reminds me now
   The glory of that dawn,
Where all the stars in reverence bow
   Before their Father's throne.

2 There Jesus sits upon the throne,
   And scatters night away,
Where all His children soon will come,
   To Him their tributes pay.

3 I soon shall join that happy throng,
   Where love does rule the place,
And with my comrades wear a crown,
   And sing redeeming grace.

4 I long to see that happy place,
   From cares and sorrows rest,
With saints and angels 'dorned with grace,
   With Jesus and His blest.

5 Where anthems of melodious strains,
   From that celestial throng,
Shall sound throughout those endless plains,
   One long, eternal song.

NO. 88.   P. M.

1 O, COME, come away,
   Thy burden is distressing.
The Lord has heard thy plaintive sigh,
   O, hear what he says:

O, leave the world alone, He cries,
Take up your cross the shame despise,
Arise, now be baptized,
   And sing, grace is free.

2 O, come, come away,
   While Jesus now is pressing;
   His yoke is easy, burden's light,
How can you stay away?
   Come while the morning dew is on,
   Who feel your souls to Jesus won,
   O, like a noble son,
     And sing, grace is free.

3 O, come, come away,
   You never shall regret it,
   You did the Savior's call obey,
And join the noble band,
   Marching where sin and sorrow reign,
   And tempting foes will try to pain
   Your happiness to lame,
     O, come and join.

4 O, come, come away,
   While we try to assist you;
   The cross may seem quite hard to bear,
But all, all is joy.
   Jesus has marked the way for you,
   And left the prints in scripture too,
   To whom your praise is due,
     O, come, come and try.

5 O, come, come away,
   The world does now despise you
   Since you have left their beaten track,
And not to them bow.

Ere soon we'll leave this world's malign,
And join in songs of grace divine,
All happiness is mine,
We'll sing as we go.

NO. 89. P. M.

1 THERE is a place below the sky
   Where Zion's children meet,
There bring their solemn vows withal,
And tell their grief and burden all,
   Nigh at the Saviour's feet.

2 There Jesus sheds the oil of grace,
   Upon this remnant small,
While all that loves will seek the place,
And spread their wants before His face,
   Their Saviour and their all.

3 His glory shines in their relief,
   While all their burdens bear,
We'll hear their sorrow and their grief,
There Jesus will be in the midst,
   Their hope and joy appear.

4 O, may I find within the place,
   A covert from the storm,
Beneath her mantle hide my face,
Not worthy there to seek her grace,
   Only in servant form.

5 Our hopes and fears we'll soon suspend,
   For nobler joys above,
Where friend holds fellowship with friend,
Where age will ne'er deform nor bend,
   Without a stammering tongue.

NO. 90. P. M.

1 I WILL arise when Jesus call,
   His name is my delight;
While on His bosom I will fall,
   He then shall speed my flight.

2 There, where I'll meet my kindred friend,
   With harps forever new;
One everlasting Sabbath spend,
   While Heaven shall ring with joy.

3 I'll rest my head on pillows made
   From downy feathers there;
While o'er my face will Jesus spread
   The choicest of his care.

4 With angel's wings shall I arise,
   And fly to worlds above;
There meet my Saviour in the skies,
   With ecstacies of love.

NO. 91.

1 PERMIT now, dear brother,
   The appellation make;
Sometime since we together
   In Jesus' name did meet.
You must permit me now to say,
The hand of God does on me lay;
   While pressing down with fear,
   I will His name revere.

2 Long time I lived in sadness,
   And mourned my wretched state;
But God did cheer with gladness,
   Before it was too late.

I saw the dangerous road was in,
Propelling on from sin to sin,
  By death's resistless hand,
  Which gave no outer sign.

3 But God, although unworthy,
   Gave worthiness to see,
  Through Him, who was the surety,
   The sinner's friend to me.
  Through Him my soul was made to leap
  And mourn, because I could not weep,
   His mercies was so great,
   O, could I all relate.

4 But my poor stammering lisper
   Can never speak his praise,
  Above a childish whisper,
   Throughout these finite days.
  But O, the joy awaits above,
  For all the host redeemed by love;
   One noon day shall attend,
   Where Sabbaths never end.

NO. 92.　　L. M.

1 IF Heaven be thus, O, glorious Lord,
   Why should we grovel here,
  Afraid to die and cross the ford,
   Where our possessions are?

2 Increase our faith, increase our hope,
   With joy, and love, and zeal,
  To lean upon our great support,
   Against our every weal.

3 Incline us, Lord, to seek that place,
   Where our possessions lie,

THE WANDERING PILGRIM.

Amidst the treasures of Thy grace,
Concealed by Thee on high.

NO. 93.   L. M.

PREDESTINATION.

1 Our fathers ignorant were,
   And yet they knew it all;
Their noble sons claim wisdom here,
   Superior to their skill.

2 They claim a mighty God,
   And yet no God at all;
The sinner turns him with a word,
   And gains a heaven withal.

3 And yet one step astride,
   There's danger of a fall;
Prove faithful, is the great watch-word,
   Now 'mongst the christians all.

4 Somehow mine eyes can't see
   With such poor glasses on;
If God hadn't ever loved me,
   What would my case have been?

5 Yea, did He see ere time,
   My wretched wandering state;
Ordained His only heaven-born son,
   To be my great prelate.

6 He ordered time with will,
   With all her events too;
Decreed it with His strength and skill,
   And manned with heaven's crew.

The angels wait upon,
And carries His address
Unto the chosen sons of men,
To speak His righteousness.

8 He spoke, the worlds were made,
With every living thing;
Excisions have His laws obeyed,
With summer, fall and spring.

9 He kills, He makes alive;
He plants our footsteps here;
Before His throne His lovely saints.
Worships with love and fear.

NO. 94.   C. M.

1 Thy hand, great God, unknown to us,
Created us below;
And known to Thee are all Thy ways,
With things Thy creatures do.

2 Their days are written in Thy book,
Their steps are ordered too;
Can't well exceed one little crook,
Beyond Thy will to do.

3 One will complain with sins oppressed;
Another sees no ill;
Yet all will own they have digressed,
'Tis all to do Thy will.

4 We all have different minds below,
Each sees his neighbor's ill;
While some attired in gaudy show,
'Tis all to do Thy will.

5 Beneath Thy great mysterious will,
    Lies there the hidden man;
  He's born of nobler powers divine,
    For nobler works to span.

6 He looks beyond the flight of time,
    There sees unfading joy;
  Where nature ne'er attempt to climb,
    Nor envy a seat above.

7 Nature, when God's will is done,
    Will sink from whence she came;
  Nature is nature, still the same,
    In saints or the profane.

NO. 95. C. M.

1 BUT now, says one, what will you do,
    God's wisdom to applaud,
  To prove him universal true,
    By nature and by word.

2 But stop, my friend, before you go
    Off of the hidden track;
  What was it Jesus came to do,
    The lowly and the meek?

3 Was it for sinners to redeem,
    In nature lost, undone;
  Or here to cancel every sin,
    That man in nature done?

4 The lost He came to seek and save,
    So reads the sovereign will;
  To kill, yea, more, to make alive,
    And raise to Zion's hill.

5 The captive held by error's chain,
    And dead to his estate;
  And yet inheriter of gain,
    Secured by hands of fate.

6 Jesus, our prophet, priest and king,
    Our great forerunner here;
  He marked the road for wisdom's sons
    To gain acceptance there.

7 Their inheritance above the sky,
    All chained, and staked, and bound;
  Aye, not one devil e'er could pry,
    To change one lot of ground.

NO. 96.　　C. M.

1 GOD'S law transgressed, and yet obeyed,
    Jehovah's plan concealed;
  To keep his creatures in the shade
    Of wondrous acts he's skilled.

2 God purposed and we know not what,
    Both wisdom and much skill,
  To raise up monarchs and then blot
    Their name to every ill.

3 'Twas thus to show his mighty power,
    To govern man by will;
  To raise a Joseph from the pit,
    A Sampson for to kill.

4 Yea, not one dagger can e'er strike,
    To work one single ill;
  But what the Lord the point direct,
    To work his sovereign will.

5 We see in nations and in men,
　　Some mighty freaks of power;
　While wisdom shows some hidden hand,
　　When the dread stroke is o'er.

6 He plants in some a heavenly mind
　　Of faith, and hope, and love,
　To carry on some great design
　　In regions far above.

7 Some faults Him that he does not have
　　Us all perform some noble work;
　A giant mind will always crave,
　　And from his duty lurk.

8 Some in the vision of the night,
　　Proclaim His love and power;
　Whilst others claim their means excel,
　　To reach the hidden bower.

9 Of aught revealed or unrevealed,
　　There's mystery somewhere,
　That God in nature lies concealed
　　Unto His creatures here.

10 His purposes will ripen fast,
　　Unfolding every hour;
　Unraveling wonders of the past,
　　Displayed with skill and power.

11 Mysterious God, who chose my lot,
　　O, teach me to adore;
　Yea, reconcile to every fate,
　　With blessings from Thy store.

12 Encouraged to believe my name's
　　Within Thy volume writ;

Recorded there ere time began,
Unchanged by laws of fate.

13 In that volume sealed with blood,
Ordained by heaven's decree;
Secured the chosen sons of God,
To all eternity.

NO. 97. L. M.

GIFTS AND CALLING.

1 THE shadows of one night,
Forebode my short release,
With prayer I thus addressed the Lord
For wisdom, love and grace.

2 O, may I be prepared,
To meet my God in peace;
I need this night, my Saviour, Lord,
Thy all sustaining grace.

3 And should I ne'er behold,
On earth another morn;
O, may I rise in spirit worlds,
Where darkness never come.

4 The answer was impressed,
I cannot let thee go;
A nobler work, go spread my grace
And mercy here below.

5 Dear Lord I will obey
Instruction's warning voice;
Let grace and wisdom equal be,
My hope and only choice.

NO. 98. L. M

1 A GIFT unto each saint,
   The Lord does always give;
Many or few, how strong how faint,
   It teaches us to love.

2 Public or private life,
   Command this light to shine;
No jealous fear or envious strife,
   But with a willing mind.

3 It works uniting love,
   Within the christian mind;
Not hating one another here,
   But penitent and kind.

4 It binds our souls to God,
   With cords of fervent love;
Not easy broken by a word,
   Though all the world should strive.

5 This gift is planted here,
   Within the human mind,
By God's sufficient matchless power,
   And scents the church divine.

NO. 99. L. M

1 WHEN in my youthful days,
   And wallowing in my sin,
Unthinking of my heedless ways,
   Or what a state was in.

2 Lo! some kind hand unseen,
   Conveyed the tidings down;
Made known the state that I was in,
   How wretched and undone.

3 It deepened on my mind,
  With fast enraging speed,
That I, one of the basest kind,
  Transgressed the law of God.

4 I to the law repaired,
  To see what I could do;
Against my case the pages read,
  The sinner there must die.

5 Mercy was now my plea,
  Although His justice doomed
My soul to endless misery,
  Beyond the fated tomb.

6 But with expiring breath,
  He heard my plaintive sigh,
And instantly with love applied
  Salvation from on high.

7 My load of guilt removed,
  And made me feel His power;
Yea, then I did begin to love,
  E'en from that very hour.

NO. 100. S. M.

1 I AM a stranger here,
  And shall be till I die;
Averse to all the themes I hear,
  Concerning joys on high.

2 The news I hear proclaimed,
  We have a little power,
And by obedience may gain
  A seat in heaven's bower.

3 Upon this wise some speak,
    God would be quite unjust
  To save a part and damn the rest,
    Who will not choose His trust.

4 I will admire God's word,
    Whether I stand or fall;
  To seek and save, cried Jesus Lord,
    My mission to fulfill.

5 To seek and save the lost,
    And give them life withal;
  To heal the sick and cure the lame,
    Such did the Saviour call.

6 Not many noble called,
    Not many sought his grace;
  Too humbling for the wise to fall,
    And plead before his face.

7 Within a stable born,
    A manger for his crib;
  A poor, despised Nazarene,
    Who would admire a bid.

8 Yet the poor sinner comes,
    Rejoiced to be a guest;
  His sins confess, the Saviour owns,
    For such prepared the feast.

9 O, may I now embrace,
    The Lord within my arms;
  And ever seek his wisdom, grace,
    With joy to spread his charms.

10 When I was sinking down,
    · I felt His love and power;

Released my soul from guilt and shame,
O what a blessed hour!

11 Since then some trials seen,
Confused by foes within;
His love extends to me the same
As when it first began.

12 O, may I sing His power,
When days and years are past,
Begun on earth the welcome hour
In heaven doomed to last.

NO. 101.   C. M.

1 AT Zion's hill the pilgrims meet
To worship, praise and pray;
There bow, low at the Saviour's feet,
They worship every day.

2 Some critics ask the reason why
These pilgrims never pray;
For all I know I can reply,
They constant watch and pray.

3 No fears of hell e'er mar their peace,
For Jesus is their friend;
In Him they find their zeal and trust,
His honor to defend.

4 Though some may stray and wander off,
In human wit display,
Like prodigals they shall return
With a repenting sigh.

5 Father, I've sinned, but O forgive,
Let me a servant be;

THE WANDERING PILGRIM.

Not worthy to be called a son,
I have dishonored Thee.

6 The Father sees a great way off,
And blesses with a smile;
My hand must lead, the ways are rough,
My rod thy sorrows heal.

7 In this same way the pilgrim comes
When he's trangressed the law,
In stripes the Lord pardons his crimes;
O, pilgrims come away.

8 Behold the world how they do gaze,
When they have drawn you off,
In mourning stand the church amazed
When they behold the scoff.

NO. 102.   C. M.

1 LORD, I desire with Thee to live,
Since Thou hast made me free,
With tongues that angels cannot tell
How rich Thy glories be.

2 Richer than all the Southern mines
Or California's gold,
In Thy rich treasury may I trust,
Where love nor zeal grows cold.

3 I was a bondsman bound in chains
Till Jesus made me free;
He paid the great redemption price
Upon the accursed tree.

4 He bore my sins, a galling load,
When justice did demand

To slay Thee, O my Saviour, Lord!
For me, O sinful man!

5 Nothing but love e'er brought him down
To suffer here below;
And shall I love Thee back again?
Ah, none but Thou dost know.

NO. 103. C. M.

1 THY ways are ways of pleasantness,
Thy paths are joy and love;
None travel there but sons of grace,
Who're born of God above.

2 Oft clouds of sorrow will arise
And dark their road while here,
But God will clear their darkest skies,
And bid the sun appear.

3 The glorious Son of Righteousness,
With healing in His wings,
Their every hope and care caress,
Their transport and their King.

4 Engaged to land them safe above,
When life's toiling is o'er,
Where constant songs of boundless love
Shall ring from shore to shore.

NO. 104. S. M.

O, WHAT a happy theme,
A pilgrim 'tis to be;
Among the saints he will sojourn,
His chief delight to see.

2 Affliction, 'tis their lot
   Upon this earthly ball;
They know it and they murmur not,
   For God is in them all.

3 Soon they shall meet above;
   May I be there to see,
There sing redeeming grace and love,
   O, what a company.

4 No tongue can ever tell,
   Nor pen the thought ascribe,
What loud hosannas constant swell
   The song of Jesus's pride.

NO. 105.

1 SEND forth Thy great victorious arm,
   O God of truth and love,
And bring thy children from afar
   To seek their joys above.

2 Bring them to Zion's chosen gate,
   Where pilgrims love to dwell;
The path is sure and firm and straight,
   All others lead to hell.

3 Unite them with cementing ties,
   Strong cords of love and peace,
Within the hidden breast it lies,
   Their joy and blessedness.

4 Be their support, deliverer too,
   When storms of sorrow rise;
Thine arm unseen can bring them through
   To joys above the skies.

5 Where hope and fear shall die in love,
  Unveil their Saviour's face;
  Will reign as kings and priests above,
  In robes of righteousness.

NO. 106.   C. M.

1 IN darkness once our souls were led,
    Serving the powers of hell;
  Unto Thy love, O Lord, was dead;
    Yea, thought that all was well.

2 But after that the Lord appeared
    And changed our doleful state;
  He turned our feet the heavenly way
    That leads to Zion's gate.

4 None of our works we have to plead
    That brought us in this way,
  But trusting in our Saviour's blood
    That stained the shameful tree.

5 That being justified by grace
    Our heirship sealed with God;
  E'er through our Saviour, Jesus Christ,
    We will his name applaud.

NO. 107.   S. M.

1 HOW can I praise the Lord
    With such a heart as mine,
  So prone to wander from the road
    That leads to joys divine.

2 Incline me, Lord, I pray,
    To love Thy charming name,

Thy holy precepts to obey,
  Thy ransom power to sing.

3 I know I feel at times
  Inclined to love the Lord;
Alas! some trivial thing steps in,
  No real joys afford.

4 When shall I see the day
  That sin no more annoy,
Nor prove a foe 'twixt God and me,
  My heavenly peace destroy.

5 O, let the time roll on,
  That brings the welcome day,
Where I in full perfection see
  The God that bled for me.

NO. 108.   C. M.

1 NE'ER by the sense of human wits
  Can we ascend the skies,
Nor reach the place where Jesus sits
  Unless He deigns to raise.

2 We must give up that we are lost
  Without His help afford;
Grace melts our nature down to dross,
  Faith shows a smiling God.

3 The Lord will do His work begun,
  And save the uttermost;
None are exempted by the Son,
  That views their nature crossed.

4 For all such mourners, bids them come;
  He stretches out an arm,

And says, without me there is none
Can bring the sinner home.

5 Then sure 'tis grace from first to last,
And not free agency;
'Tis grace our theme, 'tis grace we boast,
Marked out the heavenly way.

6 Grace, O how powerful is thy charms,
To work such love below,
Yet the poor creature hates and spurns
Till grace his will subdue.

NO. 109. 7s.

DOUBTS AND FEARS.

1 PETER'S faith away it gave
When he saw the troubled wave,
Crying, save me, Lord, or I
Must forever sink and die,

2 Oft does Jesus try our faith,
Rowing by the sense of sight;
Dark's our path, we lose the way,
Then we cry, dear Lord save me.

3 If the Lord our souls should leave,
Troubles would afflict and grieve;
Like old Peter we would cry:
Save me, Lord, or I must die.

4 But when Jesus stretches out
His great arm we cannot doubt;
Shows to us a wretched case,
If not bound by sovereign grace.

5 When our faith is strong can say,
  All my doubts I'll cast away;
  Sweetly praise the Saviour, Lord,
  For the blessings on us stored.

6 Perfect Peace we cannot have
  Till we get beyond the grave;
  Emblems of His power to save
  By the cords of filial love.

NO. 110. 7s.

1 BRETHREN, conflicts you must see,
  While we dwell below the sky;
  Watch, is the first password here,
  Mixed with hope and humble prayer.

2 Watch and pray and never fear,
  For the tempter's always near,
  Lurking for a sleeping post;
  If 'tis found, he tries the host.

3 In the Golden Rule confide,
  Lay all other rules aside;
  Many ways we always find
  To mislead the Christian mind.

4 Dangers often will appear
  Unsurmountable to view,
  In approaching disappear,
  Christians always persevere.

5 Soon these conflicts will be o'er,
  Saints and angels will adore,
  Heaven shall ring with ceaseless praise
  In one train of endless days.

NO. 111.   L. M.

1 MAY we in dust and ashes weep,
 And pray the Lord our hope revive;
 Bow low before the Saviour's feet,
 And praise Thee only while we live.

2 E'er live anew from day to day,
 Esteem each brother here in love,
 No cause to give, for others say,
 We're not engaged for worlds above.

3 The Scriptures say, might knowledge take,
 That we have been with Christ the Lord,
 And that we do their ways forsake,
 Obedient to the sovereign word.

4 But Oh, alas! they frequent say,
 We're not what we proffered to be;
 This often makes my feelings move,
 To censure that we do not love.

5 With great desire I often pray
 That soon we may behold the day,
 That in one band our songs may join
 To praise our glorious heavenly King.

6 No doubt this is the great bewail
 Of all my brethren, great and small,
 To see the glorious light of Zion,
 Ee'er spreading forth throughout the land.

7 That sinners might come flocking home,
 Declaring what the Lord has done;
 Fruits of repentance may they bring,
 And leaving all for Christ their King.

8 For all we can but wish and pray,
  And long to see the welcome day;
  In expectation may we wait,
  Still praying at the heavenly gate.

9 The Lord has marked the Christian road,
  And hope and comfort there he's strewed,
  Lo, here we find while marching on,
  These blessings cheer us long for home.

10 We soon shall land where prayers will cease,
   Where, in perfection, reign in peace,
   There to the Lamb shall we ascribe
   The honors of a loving bride.

NO. 112.   P. M.

1 NOW, brother, take courage in God,
  Hoping and believing His word;
  The promise stands good if begun,
  Press onward your journey for home.

2 He's promised that where he's begun
  Is able His will to perform;
  Will also lead safely on through
  Till sorrow and time is no more.

3 His purposes are wise and true,
  'Tis Him that works, both will and do,
  His truth and His liberty free,
  To plant it in you or in me.

4 But often I fear 'tis a form,
  His work in me is not begun;
  These doubts in darkness oft convey
  No real happiness in me.

5 I long here to see the Great Day,
When sorrows and doubts done away,
With Jesus forever live and reign,
Shouting His adorable name.

NO. 113. C. M.

1 O, NOW, my gracious God, I ask
  A blessing on my soul bestow;
E'er in Thy love and favor bask,
  The best of blessings that I know.

2 Come life, come death, come then what will,
  Nothing to be compared with Thee;
Now let my anxious cares be still,
  For they are trifles here to me.

3 I ask Thee not for glittering wealth,
  Nor earthly vanity or toys,
But Thy sweet love in life, in death,
  To live and reign above the skies.

4 To drink at that great fountain head,
  Where love, like many waters flow,
Where anxious cares will all be dead;
  To pain and sorrow bid adieu.

5 Dear Jesus, now, O quickly come,
  Gladly I go with Thee on high;
O, take the wandering pilgrim home,
  Where doubts and fears will never vie.

NO. 114. C. M.

1 IN the bright world of endless day,
  The pilgrims all shall meet
To praise the Lord in graceful glee
  Around the Saviour's feet.

2 Though troubles interfere and mar,
   And cause discord while here,
 Soon they shall join where is no jar,
   Nothing to wish or fear.

3 A shining light around the throne,
   Shall every Christian be
 In heaven, their everlasting home,
   To all eternity.

NO. 115.   S. M.

LOVE.

1 BEHOLD, how pleasant 'tis
   When brethren all agree;
 Each one fill up the little space
   In love and harmony.

2 Each whisper speaks of love,
   All centered in one head,
 United with the host above,
   And Christ the glory spread.

3 He is our life, our hope,
   Our everlasting all;
 Raises our dropping spirits up,
   And holds us lest we fall.

NO. 116.   C. M.

1 I WILL before Jehovah bow,
   With all His humble saints;
 Thy blessings crave, dear Lord, bestow,
   Fill up our needful wants.

2 'Twas Thee who brought us from the clay,
   And placed us on the rock;
   'Twas Thee who showed our feet the way
   That leads to Zion's gate.

3 As monuments of Thy kind love,
   We feel our need of Thee,
   Hoping we'll soon arrive above,
   Where we shall ever be.

4 And know and see each for himself
   The joys prepared above,
   That God in wisdom has prescribed
   For those He dearly loved.

NO. 117.   C. M.

1 BY God's eternal sovereign grace,
   I do behold the man;
   As through a glass I see his face
   That wrought the wondrous plan.

2 He was upon this earth awhile,
   And hung upon the tree,
   Derided there by all the vile,
   And died for you and me.

3 The work of grace He here begun,
   By His kind father given,
   Redeeming love to ruined man,
   To fit their souls for heaven.

NO. 118.

1 UNITE, my roving thoughts, unite,
   And sing a Saviour's love,
   For He it is that gives me light,
   And lifts my thoughts above.

2 For He it is that gives me breath
    To live from day to day,
And in the appointed hour of death
    Will take my soul away.

3 Away to that bright world of bliss,
    Where Jesus lives and reigns,
And all that know and taste His grace,
    Shall walk the heavenly plains.

4 Without a veil I know I'll see
    The God my soul adores,
And in one bright prolific day
    I'll gaze the heavenly shores.

5 Beyond the brightness of the sun,
    Illumined here below,
The glory of that heavenly Son
    His graces will bestow.

NO. 119.   C. M.

1 SALVATION, O, melodious sound,
    To save a wretch like me;
Applied to heal the dreadful wound,
    Of sin and misery.

2 Jesus, the name in every case,
    Delightful does appear;
Sweet is the music of His grace
    Upon the sinner's ear.

3 Direct from heaven the summons come,
    No power can stay the dart,
Piercing asunder every hope
    Within the stony heart.

4 When I was sinking down beneath
   My guilt, a galling load,
   His name was sweet in my relief,
   Proclaimed a smiling God.

5 O, may I loud proclaim that name,
   To sinners far and near;
   Thy power applied, great God of fame,
   Will reach the deafened ear.

NO. 120.   L. M.

1 MY early life, my boyhood days,
   I now look back my God to praise;
   His watchful care o'er me has been,
   My wandering ceased and brought me in.

2 I often thought that I was right,
   Without much fault at least to fight,
   And that I would some day commend,
   Turn to the fold and enter in.

3 But as my days grew on apace,
   God's matchless love and boundless grace
   Broke in my cell, destroyed my hope,
   My anchor and my only prop.

4 Showed me my standing in His sight,
   My works unfit to set me right,
   While love o'ershadowed, set at ease,
   My soul could say, my God appeased.

5 His boundless love still follows me
   While in the path of duty see;
   No dangers can molest or harm,
   Upheld by God's almighty arm.

6 Through many dangers have I run,
Seen and unseen since I've begun;
Life's narrow path Thy hand applaud,
Who can defend but Thee, my God.

7 Throughout the remnant of my days
Ne'er may I cease to speak Thy praise,
Both honor and applaud the name
'Midst all afflictions I have seen.

8 I know that I must soon depart,
Thy goodness cheers my spirits up;
I shall outride my sorrows here,
And in Thy image will appear.

NO. 121.   C. M.

1 THERE is a way for pilgrims here
    No vulture's eye hath seen,
Cast up for all God's children dear,
    And fools can't err therein.

2 This way was made in days of old,
    Safe and secure from fear;
Thy blessings, O, how manifold,
    Dear Lord to us appear.

3 When deep in nature's night we lay,
    Thy watchful care was o'er
And turned our darkness into day,
    While all our sorrows bore.

4 'Twas then this glorious way appeared
    To be our safe retreat,
While Jesus as our guardian guide
    Upheld our weary feet.

5 Dear Lord, howe'er can we repay
   The gratitude we owe;
Condemned a felon's doom to die,
   What mercy didst Thou show.

6 The very thought we must confess,
   What matchless power and love
Was treasured in Thy wisdom, grace,
   To raise our souls above.

7 O, keep us in the heavenly way,
   Thy name we will applaud,
Until we see the rising day
   Where all our joys are stored.

NO. 122. S. M.

1 ARE there no promises
   In mercy writ for me?
No rays of hope to cheer me up
   Ere I should faint and die?

2 Dear Lord, O let me fall
   Low at Thy sacred feet,
There my petitions may recall,
   Thy mercies to me mete.

3 I know Thou art e'er kind
   To those that do Thy will;
Dear Lord, I'm like the unstable wind,
   One moment can't be still.

4 I'm tossed to and fro,
   Like surging billows rise;
No real happiness below
   To cure my heaving sighs.

5 I've had a foretaste here,
   But clouds quite soon are driven,
   Divides my faith 'twixt hope and fear,
   And veils the promise given.

6 There's joy prepared above
   I cannot here express,
   Unchangeable, one stream of love
   E'er fill the heavenly place.

NO. 123.   C. M.

1 THERE is a dwelling for the good,
   A mansion in the skies,
   For all the childern of our God,
   His bidding shall arise.

2 When all His purposes below
   Their station has fulfilled,
   He will release the fettered soul
   According to His will.

3 Arise at the great welcome day
   From sorrow, sin and pain,
   Triumphantly their songs shall be,
   The Lamb for sinners slain.

NO. 124.   C. M.

AARON, THE TYPE OF CHRIST.

1 WHEN Aaron in the holiest went,
   His breastplate there was filled,
   With holy hands the engraver sent
   The names of Israel.

THE WANDERING PILGRIM.

2 This is a token great and wise,
   A greater priest should come,
   And in one day the sins erase
   Of every chosen son.

3 This priest has come, my soul rejoice,
   And with a token given,
   Did in that day my sins erase
   And meted me for heaven.

4 Now in these latter days appeared
   His wisdom, truth and grace,
   And taught me where my hope was staid
   In God, my righteousness.

5 A plan, a scheme so wise was laid,
   My tongue will fail to tell;
   How long this priesthood ere has stood
   The angels can't reveal.

6 The name of all the chosen race
   Written in the plan,
   Before this world the orbits chased,
   Or sun its courses ran.

7 Enough, my soul thy God adore
   For all His matchless grace;
   His wisdom swells the mighty store
   Of joy and love and peace.

NO. 125. 7s.

EVENING HYMN.

1 ONE more day does now expire,
   And the evening shades appear;
   God, who is our guide, we pray,
   Pardon our wanderings this day.

2 Keep us safe this night from harm
　Safely lead our souls along,
　Till our last expiring breath,
　Sweetly sing Thy name in death.

3 Not for worth that we have earned,
　Only through Thy name confirmed,
　And to Thee and Thee alone
　Are our praises due—Amen.

NO. 126.

MORNING DEVOTION.

1 LORD, in the morning Thou shalt have
　　The notes my tongue employ;
　The music of Thy name does give
　　A hope of love and joy.

2 In every thing I shall perform,
　　Thy blessings shall implore;
　Vouchsafe to keep me from all harm,
　　While none but Thee adore,

3 Through every period of my life
　　Thy mercies have I seen,
　Guided my wandering footsteps right
　　From every hurtful sin.

4 When death and sin shall no more reign,
　　I shall possess above
　A life quite clear from every sin,
　　And free from selfish love.

5 Where fears and foes can ne'er possess
　　That sweet unsullied joy,
　The music of Thy name suffice,
　　My every thought employ.

NO. 127.   S. M.

SABBATH.

1 THIS day is set apart
    For worship so divine;
Then let us join in hand and heart
    To praise the Saviour's name.

2 In one harmonious strain
    Let no discords arise;
As children of the heavenly King
    May our devotion rise.

3 High to the Father's throne
    In anthems let us sing,
For unto Him our wants are known,
    Our universal King.

4 With grace He will supply,
    And feed the heavenly mind;
With streams of love His name convey,
    And scents the Church divine.

5 This Sabbath soon will close,
    And others hasten on;
The children of our King shall see
    An everlasting one.

6 When in perfection rise,
    Shall see that heavenly day,
As orbients of these lower skies,
    Our King His saints array.

7 Adorned in robes of love,
    Shall every Christian be;
Forever reign with Christ above
    In all eternity.

NO. 128. C. M.

SEASONS.

1 O, HOW refreshing is the rain
   Has fallen here this day;
Makes every plant revive again,
   Fast withering away.

2 O, Lord of heaven and Lord of earth,
   That scatters this rain down,
O, give us hearts of gratitude
   To accept the favor shown.

3 Send down upon each heavenly mind
   A shower of quick'ning grace;
Within Thy glorious presence find
   A seat of love and peace.

4 Yea, would Thou from this hour begin,
   Thy glorious work renew;
And may each plant revive again
   In Zion confirmed anew.

5 We fear unless Thou soon return,
   Each plant will droop and die;
Permit us not to droop again,
   Return Thou from on high.

6 The soul that waits on Thee shall live
   By Thy kind guardian care;
From day to day his wants relieve,
   Thy mercy ne'er forbear.

NO. 129.   P. M.

1 THE changing seasons tell us
    That winter's drawing nigh;
The foliage of the summer
    Is withered up and dry.
Ah, soon will youth divested be,
The bloom of life a summer's tree
Whose mantle is soon gone;
Old age is creeping on.

2 But O, disease invade us,
    The young, the old must die;
Could not some angel guard us
    When the dread monster's nigh?
But O, our time allotted 'tis,
He cannot touch until it please!
The God that called us here;
Our time to us is dear.

3 Could not some angel teach us
    That when we're called to die,
That happiness awaits us
    Above the lurid sky?
The joyful news would cheer us up,
With gladness take the bitter cup,
And long the time to come
When we should be at home.

4 But O, the moment's flying,
    And we run heedless on;
The season will be trying,
    Without a robe to don.
The Saviour has a glorious robe
For all the chosen sons of God,

Wrought out on Calvary's tree:
O, let me go and see.

5 The welcome news, come follow,
   Take up your cross, despised
By all the sons of sorrow,
   Arise and be baptised;
My sons must willing subjects be,
There willingness they'll find in me;
I've grace for every need,
Come taste and you are freed.

6 Released from sin and sorrow,
   Inspired by faith and hope,
To look upon the morrow
   Where winter storms are broke,
Where warmest rays will ever shine
From that eternal Son divine,
Where changing seasons o'er,
And sorrow comes no more.

NO. 130.   C. M.

1 HOW shall I see that happy place,
   And be forever blest?
'Tis through my Saviour's smiling face,
   The invitation rest.

2 He spreads the glorious news around
   To dying sons of men,
And all that hear the welcome sound
   Shall seek the pardoning Lamb.

3 Nor shall they seek the Lord in vain,
   For He is always near;

A deafened ear will never turn,
Though trembling come with fear.

4 O, may I come with faith inspired,
There plead my sins forgiven
Through the atoning lamb of God,
The only hope of heaven.

NO. 131.   L. M.

AFTER SERMON.

1 NOW let us all depart in peace,
And treasure up what we have heard; ·
In honest hearts let truth and grace
Receive these blessings from the Lord.

2 In prayer and faith now ask the Lord
To pardon all that's said amiss,
While truth and hope attend the word
To sanctify our future bliss.

NO. 132.   C. M.

1 CENSURES we'll gain while dwelling here
Upon the beaten track;
Our foes like mountains does appear
To drive our courage back.

2 Applause will come from friends most dear,
These earthly passions move;
Our nature will assuredly bear
Towards the objects loved.

3 Dear Lord, O may I prove quite deaf
To censure and applause;
They spring from nature, their relief,
And will not change my cause.

NO. 133. C. M.

1 WHY is it thus with me, O Lord?
  No spark of gratitude,
  No cheering rays Thy word afford
  To rouse my sleeping mood.

2 O, why should I here lull to sleep
  Where dangerous foes abound,
  And meteors of glaring speed
  Burst over all the ground.

3 Give me a heart of feeling sense
  Thy goodness to implore,
  In Thee to feel a sure defense;
  I cannot ask for more.

NO. 134. C. M.

1 WHEN I survey the wondrous cross
  On which the Saviour hung,
  It leads my mind to search the cause,
  The Lamb for sinners slain.

2 Determined by Jehovah's will,
  This day ordained to come,
  That God is God and righteous still,
  The Lamb he must be slain.

3 Ere time began the scheme was laid
  To rescue fallen man;
  For by Jehovah's will 'twas made,
  The Lamb he must be slain.

4 Their wicked, trembling hearts gave way,
  When seen what they had done;
  'Twas for such sinners, Lord, as I,
  The Lamb he must be slain.

Our souls immersed in deepest hue,
In darkness must remain;
And to release the vengeance due,
The Lamb he must be slain.

6 He hung upon the wretched cross
Our pardon to maintain;
To pay the great redemption price,
The Lamb he must be slain.

7 O, may we now with sweet accord
E'er join to praise His name;
To praise our gracious sovereign Lord,
The Lamb for sinners slain.

NO. 135.   P. M.

1 COME, undone and needy sinner,
    Christ can heal your vilest wounds;
He's the man, our great Redeemer,
    Brought us from distress and bonds.
Streams of mercy every hour
    Constant from His wounds do flow:
Come and taste His saving power,
    There is mercy yet for you.

2 Lo, He stands, and always waiting
    To receive the sin-sick soul:
Come and try, though almost fainting,
    None but Christ can make thee whole.
He can cause the lame to walk,
    And, yea more, the blind to see,
Loose the stammering tongue to talk;
    What a kind Saviour is He.

3 He's the Christian's hiding place;
    Their defense from gathering storms;

Bound in chains of love and peace,
  Gently gather with His arms.
In one fold He'll bring them safe,
  Each arrayed in robes of love,
Far beyond this world of grief,
  Safe on yonder shores above.

NO. 136. C. M.

1 IN Thee, O Lord, I put my trust,
   My hope it is in Thee;
 Keep me in paths of righteousness,
   Incline thine ear to me.

2 Thou art my hope, even from my youth,
   O, guard me till I die;
 Let not Thy mercy and Thy truth
   Ever to pass me by.

3 Thou hast e'er held me up till now,
   And will until I die,
 Will be my portion here below,
   And mine above the sky.

NO. 137. C. M.

DIVINE WORSHIP.

1 LORD, bless the assembly waiting here,
   With blessings from Thy hand;
 Fill all our hearts with love and fear,
   As brothers of one band.

2 Thou knowest our wants and weak desire;
   Incline our hearts to pray,
 With Thee prevailing would implore
   A blessing here to-day.

3 Give each to understand Thy law
   With sweet delight to run,
To praise Thee, Lord, from day to day,
   Until our setting sun.

4 Bring us to see Thee face to face,
   Without a vail between,
Where foes can't harm or fears molest,
   Be endless praises Thine.

NO. 138.   C. M.

1 MAY we in sweet devotion join,
   Each saint assembled here,
Tuning the voice to sing Thy praise
   In love and holy fear.

2 Make this assembly, Lord, to feel
   'Tis good that we are here;
O melt our hearts, though hard as steel,
   While in thy courts appear.

3 Upright and just, O Lord of host,
   We would rejoice to be,
But sins oppress, our way oppose,
   And frights our souls away.

4 O drive these faults forever way,
   That we may worship Thee
In peace unto that perfect day,
   Where shall no hindrance be.

5 There where the Lord our Saviour reigns,
   And shows a smiling face,
Preparing mansions for His Lambs,
   Redeemed by sovereign grace.

NO. 139.   S. M.

1 O GOD of truth and love,
    Teach my poor soul to pray,
  And pray in faith of joys to come
    Of that immortal day.

2 I am a stranger, Lord,
    A wanderer here below,
  And what I am I find 'tis hard
    On earth for me to know.

3 Sometimes I feel inclined
    To love Thee if I could;
  But often feel another mind,
    Averse to all that's good.

4 Incline me more and more
    To love Thee, Lord, I pray;
  Yea, constantly Thy name adore
    In this declining day.

5 And when my race is run,
    Confirm me with a word,
  That I shall meet a smiling face,
    The glories of my Lord.

NO. 140.   C. M.

1 HOW sad by nature is our state,
    When we behold within,
  Pollutions much our souls abase
    With grief and shame and sin.

2 Escape impossible appear
    To our bewildered eye,

While loaded down with shame and fear,
To us all hope despair.

3 Then with an humble, contrite heart,
Will our petition rise
To God to set our souls apart
From vanity and lies.

4 How much rejoiced we find with bliss
To see our prayer returned
With wisdom, truth and every grace,
By faith and hope confirmed.

5 With thankful hearts and graceful songs,
We will address the Lord;
To Him our happiness belongs,
Who has our wills subdued.

NO. 141.   L. M.

MEN'S WORKS COMPARED WITH GOD'S.

1 HOW will the sons of men appear,
Compared with Jesus' word,
Claiming to preach the Gospel here,
And leading souls to God?

2 Portraying by their measures here,
Whole nations are restored.
Without their aid they claim, they fear,
Would never see the Lord.

3 Compare their works with Holy Writ,
And see what they have done,
Portrayed that God does truly sit
On a precarious throne.

4 They claim if means and measures used,
   God's house will soon be full;
   But slackened hands among the Jews
   Sends thousands down to hell.

5 I give to them eternal life,
   So says the holy Word;
   And all the Father giveth me
   Shall surely seek the Lord.

6 Ye must be born, He said, again,
   Or ye can't see the Lord;
   Born not of blood, nor will of man,
   But by the will of God.

7 All that the Father give to me
   Shall come to Zion's hill;
   One garment there not needed be,
   Not one but some one fill.

NO. 142. 7s.

1 NEARER to our home above
   Every moment here we come;
   Selfish nature soon will be
   Resting in the silent tomb.

2 Freed from earthly care and toil,
   Raised from transitory things,
   Join the happy throng withal,
   Stand amazed at the bright scenes.

3 Stand amazed, be God adored,
   At the splendor there prepared;
   By his hands for us is stored
   Joys the world cannot afford.

4 Grace and wisdom meekly shine,
    While the heavenly arches ring;
    Praise and honor, Lord, are Thine,
    Sound the echoed notes we sing.

5 Come what will, I'm now prepared;
    By Thy grace I sweetly sing;
    Raise me to that house, O Lord,
    There to dwell with Christ, my King.

NO. 143.   C. M.

1 BY ties of nature and of God,
    We feel a nearness here;
    O, happy souls! it is the Lord
    That drives away our fear.

2 'Tis by the Lord our souls are fed,
    By grace and wisdom given;
    By faith we see his promise spread,
    Revives the hope of heaven.

NO. 144.   P. M.

1 BRETHREN, ye who have the pleasure
    Meeting with the saints of God,
    There replenishing your treasure,
    Which does come from His abode.
    Ye who meet below together,
        Pray for those that cannot come;
    Pray their malady recover,
        They who trust in Jesus's name.

2 Sin and sickness and much sorrow
    Vails the heavenly mind below;
    But our faith looks on the morrow,
    Where unclouded joys we view.

Pray the Lord, who 'tis forgives us,
  He that guides our steps below;
In His goodness still direct us
  To the haven which we go.

3 Pray the Lord to ease affliction
  By His presence to the saints;
Kindle up a soft affection
  By supplying all their wants.
Pray for faith that when we're dying
  We may look beyond the vale;
Look to Jesus, all supplying,
  And in Him the victory hail.

NO. 145. C. M.

1 BLEST with the smiles of love and grace,
  By our loved Jesus given;
There will our troubles greet with peace;
  O, what a blessed heaven.

2 Yea, will the heavenly arches ring,
  When all that kindred rise;
Redeemed by grace will ever sing
  Above these gloomy skies.

NO. 146. C. M.

1 HAPPY the heart where grace inspire
  To move with heavenly seal;
Love is the bright and morning star
  That works the sovereign will.

2 The heart inspired by hope and fear,
  To gaze on Zion's hill;

Almost forgets her sorrows here,
And longs with God to dwell.

3 Our joys are but a feeble sight,
Poor nature cannot bear
To see the soul enrobed in light
While she in dust appears.

4 But soon we'll drop this dying flesh
To reap our joys above,
Where faith o'erwhelmed in heavenly bliss
Shall sing that God is love.

NO. 147.   C. M.

1 VAIN world begone with all your joys,
You have no charms for me;
I've tasted of your subtle flowers,
Each sweet I find a snare.

2 I ask for joys above the skies,
Where Jesus sheds abroad
The glory of my brightest days,
The honors of my God.

3 I only ask below the skies
To live upon my Lord,
And trust in His rich promises
Found in the sacred word.

4 My hope is centered far above
Where sorrows never come;
Where Jesus, by His filial love,
Makes heaven a happy home.

NO. 148.   C. M.

1 The soul that loves is born of God,
　For God himself is love;
　'Tis love ensured our lively hope,
　And raised our thoughts above.

2 While sinking down beneath our load
　The love of God appeared;
　He that begetteth is the Lord,
　'Tis He our souls inspired.

3 What love, amazing love is this
　That gave us heaven below,
　Renewed the soul, engaged our bliss,
　Where faith and hope may grow.

NO. 149.   C. M.

1 JESUS, I love Thy charming name,
　'Tis suited to mine ear;
　When I was poor, and blind and lame,
　Thy mercies did appear.

2 My heart was rich in worldly goods,
　I had no need for more,
　'Till Jesus took away my prop,
　When all my strength gave o'er.

3 But in His goodness gave a heart
　To feel my wretched case;
　My sins were piercing like a dart,
　Destroying all future bliss.

4 While in a wretched, dying state,
　Thy goodness I adore;

Dear Jesus, could I ever speak,
Thy mercies ne'er explore.

5 O, for Thy wisdom and Thy grace,
To spread Thy charming name;
Amidst Thy noble chosen race
I will rehearse Thy fame.

NO. 150.   C. M.

1 HOW condescending and how kind,
That God for us prevailed,
Enrobed in flesh the heavenly mind,
Our haughty foes assailed.

'Tis He by His almighty love
Gives us relief below,
And through the image of His Son
Receives our homage now.

3 When we were dead to all that's good,
Enwrapt in nature's night,
Justice drew forth her dreadful sword
And fell on His delight.

4 He' fell, but fell to rise again,
For us He bore the stroke;
He fell, the lamb for sinners slain,
While all our sorrows took.

5 Our grievances were laid on Him
That we might be reprieved,
And find a balm for every sin
Through the deep wounds received.

6 Dear Lord, how free, how rich Thou art,
To undertake our case;

What condescending love to embark
In such a glorious cause.

7 Our confidence is firm in Thee,
 The cause engaged is sure;
 Thy mercy is our only plea;
 We'll to the end endure.

8 Yes, when this mortal life shall cease,
 We shall possess above
 A life engaged in endless peace
 To sing redeeming love.

NO. 151. S. M.

1 O, BLESS the Lord, my soul,
 For He's immensely good;
 His mercy reaches to my case
 In every time of need.

2 Although prostrate I lay,
 Under afflictions pant,
 He makes his visits every day
 And looks up all my wants.

3 O, may I ne'er forget
 The mercies of my God;
 E'er from my lips his goodness speak,
 And spread His praise abroad.

NO. 152. L. M.

1 ATTEND, my soul, upon the Lord,
Obedience to His sovereign word;
He calls for thee, thy cross to take,
And follow in the paths He's made.

2 His burden's easy, yoke is light,
  His precepts good, His ways are right;
  Clear from all harm shall ever be
  The souls, says Jesus, follows me.

3 All other paths will lead astray,
  And lead the soul from endless day;
  Ah, Lord, how shall I follow Thee,
  'Midst all the callings here I see.

4 Dear soul, rely upon my word,
  Obey the honors of thy Lord,
  And where He calls for thee to go,
  Submission to His precepts show.

NO. 153.   L. M.

1 THERE is a way to men seems right
  But leads us down to endless night;
  While narrow is the holy way
  That leads us up to endless day.

2 The one is run by our free will,
  Dependent on the human skill,
  While God declares, ye shall be brought
  In paths ye never hath sought out.

3 A way that leads from banishment,
  The way the holy prophets went;
  And Jesus proves the way is good,
  Dying as man and raised as God.

4 'Tis through His name ye must be brought,
  And all that come will not cast out;
  Our works of righteousness will be,
  Hear what the Lord has done for me.

NO. 154.   C. M.

1 MY days on earth, O may I spend,
   In truth and wisdom's ways;
  The honors of my Lord defend,
   Withal to speak His praise.

2 Riches nor honor do I seek,
   I leave them to the world,
  But be a follower of the meek,
   His glorious banner hurl.

3 Jesus inspire my lonely breast,
   Thy goodness to adore,
  Until I come unto that rest
   Prepared in days of old.

4 'Tis nothing but Thy wisdom, Lord,
   Will make me mete for heaven,
  And through Thy righteousness adored
   My sins were all forgiven.

5 Wisdom and truth and virtue shine
   Through Thy unuttered ways;
  Justice and honor in each line,
   Spread forth Thy glorious praise.

NO. 155.

1 COME, O thou sons of God, proclaim,
   And sing of Jesus' love;
  Sing of His matchless power and fame
   That raised our thoughts above.

2 Sing of His love when all was gone,
   Our souls gave up in gloom;
  Sing of His power when we had none,
   And sinking down at noon.

3 Sing how He intercedes for us,
   And gave us nobler birth,
   W... ... ...
   His mighty power brought forth.

4 Sing how H...
   The ... ...
   When in a moment reached our p...
   And raised our spirits up.

5 Sing what His love has been since then,
   When troubles pressed us down,
   While all along the road has been
   The presence of His arm.

6 Sing on, dear dying souls, sing on,
   Heaven's almost in view;
   Then loud we'll sing and harp again,
   More clear and sweeter too.

7 A nobler song there's none can sing,
   No angels can describe;
   Although they dwell around their king,
   Can't sing that Jesus died.

8 Sing on, ye ransomed of the Lord,
   Your crown appears in view;
   And then you'll sing more clear, more loud,
   That Jesus died for you.

NO. 156. C. M.

1 ON Calvary's mount a river runs,
   A stream of milk and wine,
   While there the race of Israel's sons
   Will drink the flowing stream.

2 It shall their every want supply,
   With medicine and food;

Its healing virtues they defy
The world to supersede.

3 Its good to cleanse the foulest stains
   That sin in us have made;
And there we drink, and drink again,
   Nigh at the fountain head.

4 This stream will not at all run dry,
   E'er while we sojourn here,
There drink and drive our wants away
   Unto the rising day.

5 No lion's whelps can ever tread
   Within its sacred ebb,
Nor vulture's eye nor beast of dread
   Has seen the flowing tide.

6 It ever flows from Jesus' veins
   For dying sons of men,
While love does greet the rising winds,
   To fill the heavenly ground.

NO. 157.   L. M.

1 HOW could my soul deny the Lord,
Since all my boast is in His word,
His care is over me by night,
And all my strength by morning light.

2 He brought me by a way knew not,
And led in paths I had not sought;
My darkness fled, the light revealed
The Son of God, my hope and shield.

3 'Tis thus will every sinner boast,
   Renewed in heart and saved by grace;

I'll praise the Lord in whom I trust,
He is my all, my righteousness.

4 He is the bright and morning star,
The one that Jacob's sons prefer ;
Though Jacob's sons did boast their lot,
Yet Israel's God was their support.

NO. 158. L. M.

OMMEMORATION OF THE LORD'S SUPPER.

1 AROUND Thy table, Lord, we come
For to commemorate Thy name ;
O, that each humble heart may view
Thy shameful death and sufferings too.

2 And while we eat the broken bread,
In memory of our risen head,
O, may we search our hearts and see
If e'er we did the Lord betray.

3 The great inquiry once was made,
Beneath the winter's evening shade,
Lord, is it I ? Lord, is it I ?
My Lord and Master will deny.

4 We eat the bread and drink the wine,
And feel the effects of love divine ;
In imitation let this be done,
At the appointed hour He'll come.

5 Then in Thy kingdom new we'll eat,
And of Thy richest dainties take ;
Our banquet there will ever be,
O Lord may I be there to see.

NO. 159   C. M.

THE SAFETY OF THE CHURCH.

1 THERE is a place where Jesus reigns
   Above these lower skies,
While here His choice in waiting stands
   Till He shall bid her rise.

2 Exalted though he reigns above,
   His watchful care is o'er
The church, His bride, His faithful love,
   For those whose sins He bore.

3 Her righteousness she pleads
   Through Jesus' bleeding veins,
While He is all the strength she needs
   To build her hopes upon.

4 He is her fortress and her tower,
   To shield her from the storm,
While o'er her person constant shower
   His richest blessings down.

5 O, blessed state are they who fill
   Her earthly courts below,
Where richest dews of heaven distill
   Their grace and wisdom too.

NO. 160.   S. M.

1 O, MAY I ever find
   In Thy fair palace, Lord,
A place to rest my wearied limbs
   In honor to Thy word.

2 An humble, contrite heart,
   Affectionate and kind,

Sincere in truth in every part,
A copy, Lord, of thine.

3 My days are few indeed,
Convert them to Thy use;
And when they are accomplished here,
Receive in heaven at last.

4 Where all my joys await
For pleasures ever more,
Stand ready at the heavenly gate,
I'll triumph and adore.

NO. 161.   L. M.

1 NOW let us all unite to praise,
With thankful hearts our voices raise
To bless the day that gave us birth,
And triumphed in a Saviour's worth.

2 Each heart will now His love proclaim,
Whene'er they read on every line
His goodness and His truth impress,
He is the Lord, our righteousness.

3 He is the Lord, our keeper too,
And works in us both will and do;
Then let us mind, observe His ways,
And yield obedience to His laws.

4 In Him we live and move, anon,
And through Him all our blessings come;
O, happy day, I still must say,
The day He showed our feet the way.

5 With willing accents let us prove,
The truth and wisdom of His love;

Nor ever want a tongue to spread,
The richest merits of our Lord.

6 These flying moments soon will cease;
Dear Lord, may we depart in peace,
To meet in Zion, keep the feast
Prepared for all the heavenly host.

NO. 162. P. M.

THE SINNER'S FRIEND.

1 COME humble souls to Jesus,
   And learn to follow Him;
'Tis by His grace He frees us
   From malady and sin.
'Tis by His power our foes are chased,
And by His will our hopes are based;
Through all my life I see
He is the friend for me.

2 O, may I ever follow,
   And at His bidding go;
He will support through sorrow,
   And strong temptations too.
Come, pilgrims, lean upon His staff,
Surely He'll stand in your behalf,
Though wolves around me prey,
He is the friend for me,

3 I find Him here in sickness,
   A friend in time of need;
Although I sink in weakness,
   His hand supports my head.
His presence stifles all my pain,
With such a friend I can't complain;

Through trials plain I see
He is the friend for me.

4 When death my life shall sever,
　My faith is firm and strong;
　He will His faithful gather,
　And hide them from the storm.
　Ah, none shall suffer loss indeed;
　Whom Jesus' love has ever freed
　His shining courts shall see—
　He is the friend for me.

NO. 163.   L. M.

THE WANDERING PILGRIM.

1 I AM a wanderer below,
　And what I am 'tis hard to know;
　My mind caressed with hope and fear,
　When will my journey's end draw near?

2 The path I tread is firm and straight,
　But sore temptations often bait,
　In soft disguise allure my feet
　To turn aside, vain trifles greet.

3 'Tis then I find my weakness out,
　And pray the Lord to turn about,
　Give me the pilgrim's path to tread,
　Withal the pilgrim's guide to lead.

4 His presence will my wanderings chide,
　And bid me shelter near His side:
　There all my hopes and fears caress,
　He is the Lord, my righteousness.

5 His presence sweetens every breath,
A light to shine upon the path,
Will safely guide through woe and weal,
Up to the gates of Zion's hill.

6 These bars will at His bid unclasp,
To let the weary pilgrim pass,
Safely in heaven be at home,
While angels sing, a pilgrim's come.

7 Bright scenes will there arouse the mind,
Such perfect happiness to find;
Our sorrows dropped beneath the vale,
While fears and hope no more bewail.

8 The happy day will soon appear,
When pilgrims shall the welcome hear;
Your Father calls, come to the feast,
Where wearied pilgrims all are guests.

9 When we've been there ten thousand years,
The pilgrim's song more bright appears;
Amazing grace, how rich, how free,
'Twill last to all eternity.

NO. 164. P. M.

1 A LITTLE hope I have,
　In Jesus crucified;
It was my soul to save,
　The Father glorified,
That Jesus came to seek and save
Poor sinners 'neath an awning wave.

2 A little hope I have,
　The Father will not chide,
Nor let the billowed wave

The glorious pattern hide;
Jesus the pattern once was given,
He showed our feet the road to heaven.

3 A little hope, I say,
   To every pilgrim given,
'Twas in that blissful day
   He found the road to heaven:
O happy day, must say, indeed,
When from thy sins and guilt was freed.

4 A little hope, indeed—
   But strong enough to last
Until the soul is freed
   From every stormy blast—
When sin and sorrow will release,
And I shall see my God in peace.

NO. 165.   S. M.

1 AND do I follow Thee?
   Behold me, Lord, and see;
Or am I carried to and fro
   By my own vanity?

2 And do I love thee, Lord?
   Behold my heart and see;
Each idol in my bosom stored
   Now separate from me.

3 O let me worship Thee
   In holiness and fear,
In singleness of heart should be
   My great devotions there.

4 O let me worship Thee,
   And if I've not begun,
O help me to begin to-day
   Before the setting sun.

5 O let me worship Thee
   In songs of grace divine;
Pour forth, my soul, thy grateful glee—
   The Lord is ever thine.

6 O, Lord, now hear my prayer!
   Give utterance to tell
Whether alone or with the saints
   'Tis with the righteous well.

7 'Tis well when joys arise,
   Or when we weep and pray;
And 'tis as well when sorrows rise
   To fright our souls away.

NO. 166.   C. M.

1 THEY led Him forth to Calvary's brow,
   With language of disdain—
"Ah! prophecy who struck Thee now,
   O thou mysterious man.

2 "We have you now within our power,
   To buffet and rebuke."
So said the Jews in that lone hour
   When they the Saviour took.

3 With gorgeous robe and thorny crown
   They did the Lord array;
With cruel nails His flesh was torn,
   While friends fled far away.

4 Think, O my soul, e'er could it be
    You took a willing part,
  Your sins help nail Him to the tree—
    'Twas they that pierced his heart.

5 For you He bore the galling load
    Of sin and misery,
  To pacify a transgressed law
    Betwixt thy God and I.

6 O love, amazing love was this,
    That brought the Saviour down,
  To fall a victim to our vice
    And raise us to a crown.

7 Dear Lord! how can I e'er repay
    The honors of Thy name,
  While all the glories of that day
    Shall be to God the Lamb.

8 O may I hide beneath the cross,
    While he my case proclaim,
  And count it grace, yea all free grace,
    If I His merit gain.

NO. 167.   C. M.

1 PIERCED me ye railing sinners stood,
    While trickling down the blood
  Foretold ye did not know the Lord,
    Or your Redeemer God.

2 My soul must sink beneath the load,
    The wrath of God will tell,
  Eternal banishment becomes
    My soul exceeding well.

3 But O the dreadful thought depart!
    Is more than I can bear;
  Lord! can'st Thou touch a rending smart!
    O can'st Thou hear my prayer!

4 But if I perish I will pray,
    And fall beneath Thy cross,
  While torrents from my eyes portray
    It is the Lord I've lost.

5 Perhaps He may admit my plea
    To fill a servant's place,
  Not worthy in His presence be,
    While shame covers my face.

6 Me thinks I hear His lovely voice:
    "Poor soul, I all forgive,
  For you I bore the painful cross,
    That your poor soul might live."

7 What cheering news it is to hear
    The Saviour's pard'ning voice;
  It kills our sorrow, quells our fear,
    And makes the soul rejoice.

NO. 168. C. M.

1 THIS is a day in which our prayers
    Should well ascend the sky,
  Our harps with ceaseless songs prepare
    To bring the Saviour nigh.

2 Deceivers and deceptions rage,
    With high uplifted hand,
  Spreading their voice through every age,
    As well through every land.

3 They tell us that the Saviour died
    And canceled every sin,
While all that's left can be denied,
    There's room to enter in.

4 The choice, they say, belongs to man—
    To choose or let alone,
To climb the heavenly field and scan,
    Or sink beneath a frown.

5 They own a little they may fall,
    And lose the great reward;
Their faith and hope is centered all
    In them, and not the Lord.

6 In faith and works the Lord deny
    His power to turn the will,
Unless the soul his sins descry
    And turns from every ill.

7 Dear Lord, if this is Christian food
    I must forever die;
O teach my heart to know the good,
    And on Thy name rely.

8 I know in Thee, O Lord, is power
    To cast me down to hell,
Or raise me to that heavenly bower
    Where grace and wisdom dwell.

9 I read the choice is made with Thee,
    By faith it is revealed,
And that Thine eye alway foresee,
    Thy grace our hearts have sealed.

10 Grace teaches the poor soul to pray
    The Lord his hope secure,
While faith enables him to say
    The Lord will answer prayer.

11 I know that if I'm ever saved
   'Tis more than I deserved;
Thy power and name will ever have
   The glorious praise preserved.

12 With thankful heart and cheerful tongue,
   O may I speak Thy name,
And give the praise where praise belongs,
   While life and breath remain.

13 And when my life and breath shall cease,
   O may I then possess
A life of endless joy and peace
   In Thee my Righteousness.

NO. 169. C. M.

1 BEHOLD! I see a lady fair,
   All decked in needle work;
A king's daughter cannot compare
   In works of nature wrought.

2 I ask thee now who decked thee so?
   From whence thy beauty came?
No mortal power could make a show,
   Or thy display arraign.

3 Those ornaments are rich, indeed,
   With chains of finest gold;
Thy steps are ways of graceful speed,
   Too joyful to be told.

4 Thy bracelets and thy earrings, too,
   The crown upon thy head,
Sets thee above a princess' view—
   In beauty thou'rt arrayed.

5 Now listen to the tale I tell—
My history will be given:
I am a lady and a belle,
Prepared for joys in heaven.

6 There was a time when I was poor,
My nakedness I saw;
In filth and rags I wandered far—
My case was one of woe.

7 I felt that I was deaf, indeed—
My tongue was silent too;
I mourned the day that I was born,
And bound in sin and woe.

8 I felt that I was deep in debt,
And not wherewith to pay;
Deeply oppressed with shame and grief,
Thus lived from day to day.

9 While wandering in the open field
The king's son passed me as I roved;
The presence of his glory filled
My heart with filial love.

10 My nakedness his skirt did hide—
His robe became me well;
With water, then, my filth assayed,
Anointed me with oil.

11 Sure this was then a time of love—
Oh happy, happy day;
Cleansed of my guilt and well approved,
None can my rival be.

12 The King, his presence shadowed forth—
My Son I well approve;
The covenant made 'twixt thee and me
This day is sealed with love.

13 'Tis bound in bands no power can break,
   Combined with iron zeal;
 I am the Lord—this oath I make:
   All things hath been done well.

14 Behold thy bride! no spot in her,
   Enwrapped in broidered work;
 Her girdle made with linen fair,
   With silk most glorious wrought.

15 Her bracelets and her golden chains
   Sets forth a lovely hue;
 While on her head the crown remains,
   With all her jewels too.

16 These ornaments are nothing more
   Than gems of purest gold,
 Prepared by God the bride adore;
   'Twas made in days of old.

17 In tokens of His kind regard
   Are these rich emblems given;
 Far greater are her riches stored
   Up to her courts in heaven.

18 What must be said about that house
   Prepared for her above?
 These earthly emblems but a taste
   To show a bridegroom's love.

19 Her mansion there, most glorious wrought,
   Inlaid with precious gold,
 With cunning hands materials sought,
   To build this house withal.

20 The Father and the Son are one
   In power and majesty;
 The Bride united with the Son
   In love and unity.

21 Cemented, then, they stand as one;
    No earthly power can strew
Dissensions or discord between
    God and His chosen two.

22 E'er while He lives the Church shall live,
    Adorned with love and grace;
Beyond this earthly mansion find
    A place of joy and peace.

23 There shall her gems of beauty shine
    More glorious than the sun,
While all the heavenly host will join
    To praise the Father, Son.

NO. 170.   C. M.

1 RELIGION is the only theme
    Of mortals here below;
It kills to every hurtful sin,
    Where e'er it is bestowed.

2 Religion, pure and undefiled,
    Does magnify the heart;
Much happiness and peace will yield,
    And truth and grace impart.

3 Religion, then, should be our aim,
    While dwelling here below;
And while we dwell upon the theme,
    Its fairest virtues show.

4 Its powers our souls will much embrace
    In the great dying hour,
When kindred friends their help must cease,
    We'll triumph and adore.

5 Through Jesus' name we will arise,
   And in His image shine;
The glory of our brightest days
   Comes through that blissful name.

NO. 171. C. M.

1 HAPPY the heart that grace inspire
   To sing redeeming love;
The world looks on but to admire
   Our joys they cannot prove.

2 Grace is the keystone to the soul,
   Inspired by faith and zeal;
'Tis grace that makes the sinner whole,
   While faith his works reveal.

3 The world looks on with desperate awe,
   Say they, we'll wait awhile,
Trusting in God's most righteous law,
   In point of hope and will.

4 Their faith they claim they can increase
   By exercise and prayer;
And only while they pray impress,
   The Lord will turn and hear.

5 Revealed faith they hold apace,
   Claiming they have the will
To fight their way to God in peace,
   Or sink beneath to hell.

6 I am afraid my treacherous heart
   Would never seek the Lord,
Would never choose the better part
   Of Jesus and His word.

7 Unless the Lord my soul inspire
    To run the heavenly way,
  I would the worldling's theme admire,
    And live a Pharisee.

8 O Lord! Thy truth and grace impress,
    And teach my wandering heart
  To Thee adore, my righteousness,
    My faith, and grace, and hopes.

NO. 172.   C. M.

1 THERE is a sound in heavenly chimes
    That suits the sinner's ear;
  It soothes his sorrows, heals his wounds,
    And drives away his fear.

2 His harp is tuned to sing the notes
    Of joy and love and peace,
  While every line he sings denotes
    A sinner saved by grace.

3 O, could I hear the lovely sound
    Once more, my soul would strive
  To magnify the Saviour's name,
    And sing redeeming love.

4 Without that sound my harp would fail
    To speak a Saviour's love,
  Or find the path by saints entrailed,
    That leads to joys above.

NO. 173.   C. M.

1 DEAR Lord, now tune my harp afresh
    With music of Thy name;
  All other names I pray suppress,
    That leads me from the Lamb.

2 No other name can swell my notes
 With chants of heavenly glee;
 Unless Thy name were in my thoughts,
 In vain my songs would be.

3 Thy name is all the sinner's trust,
 Who feels his sins forgiven;
 He feels no power in dying dust,
 But trust to powers in heaven.

NO. 174.

1 BY grace the soul is saved,
 Faith brings the gift to view,
 Faith works by grace to purify,
 Rehearses all anew.

2 Grace simply draws the soul
 To run the heavenly chime,
 While faith enables her to hold
 The promises divine.

3 Divinely are they given
 Where e'er they are bestowed;
 No other hope secures us heaven,
 Freely comes from the Lord.

4 Faith, hope and grace below
 Is all the Christian theme;
 Our faith enables us to know
 Our hopes are all divine.

5 Our hope revived with grace,
 By faith we view the prize,
 The soul, encouraged, onward press
 To mansions in the skies.

NO. 175.   S. M.

1 IN Judea lies the Babe!
    The Saviour of mankind,
The angel to the shepherds said,
    In Bethlehem will find.

2 The news around did fly,
    The shepherds journey made
To Bethlehem, with joy to see
    They found the holy Babe.

3 Low in a manger lain,
    Not worthy for the inn,
Ne'er did they know it was the Lamb,
    To take away our sin.

4 What innocence portrayed
    Upon his lovely brow,
The wise men of the East afraid
    To let King Herod know.

5 Herod's strong passion rose
    To take away his life,
While Joseph, at the dreadful news,
    Rose up, he and his wife.

6 To Nazareth by night,
    They with the Babe arrived
In Bethlehem, the dreadful sight,
    Not one male child alive.

7 The king was pacified
    When the decree's fulfilled;
For fear his kingdom would divide,
    The children must be killed.

8 Lo! at the age of twelve,
  A Nazarene appeared;
With wisdom, at Jerusalem,
  His mission was portrayed.

9 The Jews, astonished, said,
  Tell us who is this lad;
If he was born of noble birth,
  We'd say the son of God.

10 Not willed to own their King,
  They tried to thrust him out,
But God, in their rejections, bring
  The Gentiles in by lot.

11 And thus the Saviour grew,
  Favored by God and man,
Fulfilling all he came to do,
  By God that was ordained.

12 The Father's will fulfilled,
  With wicked hands arraigned;
Upon the Cross His blood was spilled,
  The Lamb for sinner's slain.

NO. 176. S. M.

1 O, SPOTLESS Lamb of God!
  No guilt in Thee was found;
The man of sin should now applaud,
  For you His blood did run.

2 The third revolving morn
  The grave asunder spread,
The Saviour sprang to life again,
  And rose a mighty God.

3 His mission was fulfilled,
    Poor sinners to redeem,'
  They who the Father in His will
    Remitted every sin.

4 O, may I find my name
    Annexed unto that will,
  While God, the Lamb for sinners slain,
    Might every bosom swell.

5 With soft emotions feel,
    Our God and friend adore;
  His tender passions will reveal
    To man the grief he bore.

6 His love will be made known
    To all the heirs of grace;
  He marked the way for man to run,
    And lined it for that place

7 Where God in glory dwells,
    With all the heavenly host,
  Inviting sinners through the Lamb
    To be a welcome guest.

8 O, come without delay
    Unto the glorious feast;
  Let him that heareth not deny,
    For such are welcome guest.

NO. 177.   S. M.

1 SUCH matchless love as this
    That God for sinners bore,
  None but a faithless heart detest,
    His crimes will not give o'er.

2 It is because he loves
   Darkness rather than light,
It is the Lord the passions move,
   And sets the man aright.

3 Unless the Lord had draw'd
   By everlasting love,
I should His glorious name abhorred,
   And in my sins still rove.

4 I cannot now express
   The gratitude I owe
To Thee, my God, my righteousness,
   To Thee, my Saviour, too.

NO. 178.   C. M.

1 SWEET was the time when first I knew
   The Saviour's pardoning voice;
Sweet to my soul the music flew,
   While all within rejoiced.

2 How sweet the memory of that name,
   That has my pardon sealed;
'Tis to my soul a heavenly theme,
   When faith my hope revealed.

3 What peaceful hours I then enjoyed,
   How sweet their memory still;
My inmost thoughts were then employed
   To do my Master's will.

4 But now I feel another mind,
   Averse to all that's good;
The world, the flesh, I feel entwined,
   Allures me from my God.

5 Oft times I feel an aching heart
   The world can never fill;
   Prone from my Jesus to depart,
   And leave fair Zion's hill.

6 With mournful steps my way retrace,
   In search of heavenly joy;
   Without the Lord reveals His grace,
   In vain my works employ.

7 How long, dear Lord, with sins oppressed,
   Shall I be wandering here,
   Sometimes rejoicing in Thy grace,
   But oftener quelled with fear?

8 O, let me feel my sins forgiven,
   A contrite heart to know,
   A guide to show the way to heaven,
   From whence my comforts flow.

9 My hope, my all, from Thee does rise,
   No other name I know,
   From whence salvation could arise,
   And hope or comfort draw.

NO. 179.   C. M.

1 O, LORD, I will Thy name extol,
   For Thou has lifted up,
   My soul exceeding low did fall,
   With blessings filled my cup.

2 Thy name shall be my only theme,
   While I have breath to tell
   How narrowly my feet escaped
   The snares of death and hell.

3 Thy name my every thought employ,
  With all the powers I have,
To tell of the great rising joy
  Springs from Thy power to save.

4 Thy name my only safe retreat,
  My confidence and hope,
With willing accents I repeat
  The goodness of the Lord.

NO. 180.   C. M.

1 THERE is a day of pure delight
  Awaiting for the saints;
Exquisite pleasure banish night,
  With all their sad complaints.

2 The glory of that day demands
  One long, perpetual song,
Ascribed to Moses and the Lamb,
  Where honor does belong.

3 O, happy day! when shall I see
  The glory of Thy dawn!
This glorious day will ever be
  Immeasurably long.

4 My happiest hours look to that day
  When all my sorrows cease;
Afflictions, pains and toils will be
  Turned into joy and peace.

5 O, who would suffer here awhile,
  In expectation live?
Kind Providence ere soon shall smile,
  And thee thy crown receive.

NO. 181.   C. M.

1 THE Church adorned with grace,
  A palace built for God,
  Within her walls he finds a place,
  And sheds His love abroad.

2 God like a bulwark stands,
  Her majesty and tower,
  No earthly power can ever rend,
  Or make her insecure.

3 O, who is like her God?
  O, who has power to save?
  Will call the nations from abroad,
  The mighty from the grave?

4 His voice shall be adorned
  With grace and love and power,
  While in her courts he treadeth down
  Those that would spoil her tower.

5 In Him her resting place,
  A shelter from the storm,
  Until the works of nature cease,
  And enemies forlorn.

6 Within her sacred gate
  O, may I find a place,
  And there with hope and fear may wait,
  A monument of grace.

NO. 182.   C. M.

1 O, JESUS! lover of my soul,
  My heart with love inspire,
  A grateful, thankful song to raise,
  Emblazed with heavenly fire,

2 Without Thee, well, I know I would
    Disdain to follow Thee;
  The world, the flesh, and Satan too
    Stands ready for a prey.

3 'Tis by Thy powerful arm I stand,
    'Tis by Thy grace I sing;
  My spirit yields at Thy command,
    The music of her King.

4 My heart incline to follow Thee,
    O draw me by Thy love;
  O may all other objects flee,
    That deigns from Thee to rove.

5 My roving powers must soon resign,
    My home is not long here;
  I have a home in heavenly climes,
    A home to me most dear;

6 A home prepared by God above,
    For every chosen son,
  Where Jesus smiles a God of love,
    And angels bear them home.

NO. 183.   C. M.

1 WHEN Jesus shall again appear
    All creature hope must flee,
  While the angelic wings will bear
    Me safely to the sky.

2 Angelic songs on harps of gold
    The heavens above shall ring,
  While all the heavenly host of old
    Shall loud hosannas sing.

3 So my enraptured soul confined,
  Can here no longer stay ;
  Hasten, ye wheels of time, around,
  And bring the welcome day.

NO. 184.   C. M.

1 AFFLICTIONS are a stormy cloud
  To fright our souls away,
  When dangers lie upon the road
  That leads to endless day.

2 They seem severe, though oft are sent
  Upon the Christian road,
  To turn us from some crooked path
  That leads us from our God.

3 Though oft these shafts fall on my road,
  They bring some signs of grace ;
  They forced the prodigal's return,
  To seek his Father's face.

4 O may I, like the prodigal,
  Go seek my Father's face ;
  Not worthy to be called a son,
  Would choose a servant's place.

5 Dear Lord ! my all now rest with Thee ;
  O may I never stray,
  Nor wander off again from Thee,
  My only hope, I pray.

6 I'll look to Thee when dangers rise :
  I know Thou wilt defend
  And guard my path against my foes,
  When they their arrows send.

7 Where foes or Thy afflicting hand
   Falls heavily on me,
   I'll trust in Thy rich promises—
   My grace equals Thy day.

NO. 185.   L. M.

1 THE powers of man or angels can
  God's matchless power nor wisdom span;
  No thought explains the Eternal Word,
  But His own will—the very God.

2 His wisdom pleased not to reveal
  His majesty or goodness tell
  How He divides the earth and sea,
  And heaven and hell his laws obey.

3 Man cannot overrun his bounds,
  Nor change one law his God expounds;
  A volume lies chained to His throne,
  Fated with all the sons of men.

4 Written by the Eternal pen,
  And sealed, no man his fate has seen;
  But to our God the fate is known—
  Whether will claim or will disown.

5 Great God! into Thy hands I fall—
  Judgment and Justice meets my soul:
  Condemned to die, who can erase,
  Unless redeemed by Sovereign grace.

6 Thy sovereign grace 'tis too profound,
  By seraphs hailed or angels bound—
  Metes judgment out to Israel's race,
  And saves them through Thy Sovereign grace.

NO. 186.   L. M.

1 WHO can withstand the powers of God,
Or fathom out what He's declared?
Thy wisdom too profound for man,
A creature of God's noble plan.

2 'Midst all the creatures of His will,
Man the most sacred of His skill,
To him fair promises did write;
But blasted by the powers of night.

3 His soul was led to run the way
That leads us down to misery;
Observed our fall, and marked the way,
And wrote in lines for us to see.

4 Set up a daysman in our path—
In him appeased was His wrath;
Through him poor sinners plead their all,
Made safer than before the fall.

5 And through His power calls us to see
What, through this man, has done for me;
When no created power could save,
The Mighty God rose from the grave.

6 He sent the powers of darkness back,
While heaven and earth their center shook.
Yes, men and foes confessed him God,
But were too proud to own the word.

NO. 187.   C. M.

1 MAN'S fall esteems him dignified,
  Until convinced of sin;
The powers of night his guilt does hide,
  'Til light reveals within.

2 The greater that the light does shine,
　　The more our sins appear,
　While faith springs up within the mind,
　　And banishes our fear.

3 Faith reconciles us to our God,
　　While grace does reign within—
　Confirms through our Redeemer's blood,
　　That we are free from sin.

NO. 188.　　　C. M.

1 O WHAT is life, with all her joys!
　　What courage, hope I gain!
　Sure each sweet moment I employ
　　Is doubled back in pain.

2 In every sweet I find a snare,
　　That makes me much abhor,
　Look forward with suspect, beware!
　　Dangers are always near.

3 Were I to sail around the globe,
　　And make the seas my home,
　The passing moments then would goad,
　　And cause my soul to mourn.

4 Great God! is this my fated doom,
　　To live a life of woe?
　O let my sun go down at noon,
　　To hush the ills I go.

5 But hush, my soul, nor dare repine,
　　What God appoints is best;
　Thy conflicts make thy virtues shine—
　　His grace will hold thee fast.

6 His grace will soften every ill,
   Sufficient for the day;
   While here thy mission to fulfill.
   Thy God 'tis best to obey.

NO. 189.   C. M.

1 IT is religion to my soul,
   To hear the sinner tell
   How Jesus cleansed and made him whole,
   And hath done all things well.

2 To hear him tell what Jesus says,
   And pleads his sins forgiven—
   Guiding his feet the heavenly ways,
   Up to the ports of heaven.

3 O Jesus! lover of my soul,
   These comforts now bestow
   Upon a wretched lingering soul,
   Who feels his need of thee.

4 No other name will do him good—
   O let me hear thy voice!
   Thou art the one, the only God,
   That makes my soul rejoice.

NO. 190.   C. M.

1 LET every one that knows the Lord,
   A joyful noise now make;
   Sing praises unto Thee, our God,
   Let Zion all awake.

2 Awake, O Zion! now awake!
   Arise thou from thy sleep!

Shake off the world's bewitching snares,
And songs of honor reap.

3 Sing praises to Our King above,
In highest strains of joy;
'Tis he that causes us to love,
And all our thoughts employ.

NO. 191. P. M.

1 THERE is a hope, a blissful hope,
Though sins oppress with pain,
Our sorrows we will soon outride,
And leave them to the ebbing tide,
'Bove sin and sorrow reign.

2 There is a time, a blissful time,
When all our fleeting joy,
Suppressed with fear, and grief and shame,
We'll drop this dying flesh behind,
And rise above the sky.

3 O happy day, when shall it come,
My soul exalted stand!
When I shall hear my Saviour's voice,
And in his image I'll rejoice—
The heavenly summit climb.

4 Where grief and sorrow ne'er oppress,
Where sickness never come—
No faltering steps, no wandering mind,
No clouds to dark, or chilling wind,
In heaven, my happy home.

NO. 192. C. M.

1 MATCHLESS and wise Jehovah is,
His eye is o'er his works;

THE WANDERING PILGRIM. 171

What majesty is e'er displayed
In earth, and seas and rocks!

2 In man, the image of his God,
'Tis too profound to tell
What was he in his stature made,
Ere sin and death he fell!

3 Both good and great excelled in
The workmanship of God;
But in one little freak of sin,
O what a dire abode!

4 O was it not the promise left,
Where would we have been hurled!
His God designs in his bereft,
The Saviour of the world.

5 His own to save a ransom gave,
Like to us, without sin,
Ordained of old for Joseph's grave,
Our hopes to usher in.

6 Yea, through His fall our hopes are raised,
To show our feet the way
That reaches far beyond our sin,
Unto that glorious day.

7 Where sin and sorrow no more reign,
Made perfect through His blood—
Here is the inheritance we gain,
When we get home to God.

NO. 193. C. M.

1 THERE is a heaven above the sky,
Prepared for all the blest,

While I am afraid to die,
  And go and be at rest.

2 Dear Lord! how can I disbelieve,
    Nor trust Thy promises,
  When Thy kind hand supplies my wants
    With every needed grace?

3 The flesh dreads the cold gaping tomb,
    Until the rising day,
  When Jesus lift a long perfume,
    The spirit longs to see.

4 His name fills every soul with joy,
    Who waiting for Him stands;
  His bidding mounts the heavenly sky,
    Propelled by angel's wings.

5 Ah! one sweet day upon that hill
    Is worth ten thousand here;
  A foretaste here does fill my soul,
    What must it be up there?

NO. 194. P. M.

1 I LOVE to dream of pleasant lands,
    In happiness to roam;
  Where verdant flowers will ever bloom,
  Where reigns one long eternal noon—
    In heaven, the pilgrim's home.

2 Me thinks I hear the angels chant
    The music of that throng,
  While every thought my heart inflame,
  To harp the glory of that name,
    In one eternal song.

3 Why should I get exalted thus,
 Where disappointments bloom?
 Caress the thought, among the just,
 That Jesus will arouse my dust
  For that eternal boon.

4 My hope inspires my tongue to tell
  The glory that I see,
 Where aged and the youth will bloom
 Above the brightness of the sun,
  One long eternal day.

NO. 195. P. M.

1 HOW condescending 'twas
  For God's eternal Son
 Our sins and sorrows to proclaim,
 Were freed through His eternal name—
  On Calvary's tree was done.

2 Thy name to sinners dear,
  Who've felt Thy pardoning love,
 Applied to cleanse their souls from guilt—
 For them Thy precious blood was spilt,
  That they might reign above.

NO. 196. P. M.

1 THERE is a house for weary souls,
  'Tis far above the sky,
 Where weary pilgrims be at rest,
 No more beneath their foes oppressed,
  And sin no more annoy.

2 Jesus, the pilgrim's friend and guide,
  Will safely bring to shore,

No more to feel the oppressive hand,
But reach in safety Canaan's land,
And sing their sorrows o'er.

3 O Jesus! condescend to be
My God, whom I adore;
With Thee shall I have ought to fear,
And in Thy image may appear,
There sing my sorrows o'er.

NO. 197. P. M.

1 A monument of mercy,
  Before my God I stand;
If justice He'd conferred me,
  In lowest hell I'd land.
But O, amazing mercy ran,
To save a trembling, sinful man,
And while condemned to die,
This mercy came to me.

2 I thought that I was better
  Than some professing men,
Until I saw the fetter
  That bound my soul in sin;
And O, it was a dreadful sight,
No way could see for my escape,
And while condemned to die,
This mercy came to me.

3 But O, amazing pity,
  That God should condescend
To ransom me, the guilty,
  Through His eternal Son;
And here His blood in rivers flowed,
To satisfy the debt I owed,

And while condemned to die,
This mercy came to me.

4 O, may I ever honor
That God that bled for me,
To save a trembling mourner
From endless misery.
I'll give myself, 'tis all that I can do;
O, may I spread the glory due,
And tell poor sinners how
This mercy came to me.

NO. 198.   C. M.

1 PRESERVE me, Lord, for in Thy name
My soul puts all its trust;
Yea, Thou art mine inheritance—
I know Thy ways are just.

2 And unto Thee will I commit,
With lifted hands in prayer,
Unto the great decisive hour,
All that I have and am.

3 I know, O Lord, that Thou art just,
Therefore will courage take
To tell Thee all my cares and griefs—
My soul will ne'er forsake.

4 And in the great decisive hour,
My spirit I'll commend;
O take me to that heavenly bower,
Where all my fears shall end.

5 When love shall in perfection shine,
Without a cloud between,
I shall behold the God, the man,
That made the promise mine.

NO. 199.   L. M.

1 THE Bible proves a sealed book,
When o'er its pages oft I look;
No charms of grace its words impart,
That suits the sorrows of my heart.

2 But when the Saviour breaks the seal,
Some portion to my mind reveal;
Then O how glorious does appear,
Though oft have read the same before.

3 It seems so glorious when I read,
And understand the paths I tread,
Though strewed with fears and trials too,
They disappear when Christ I view.

4 When I can look to heaven, my home
I feel to leave the world alone—
With rapture taste the smiles of love,
That crowns the saints of God above.

5 I long to see the glorious day,
When with my Saviour borne away
To the bright world of endless bliss,
Eternally to reign with Christ.

NO. 200.   S. M.

1 AND must this body die?
    And must this flesh decay?
My soul shall rise above the sky
    At the great judgment day.

2 The time appointed 'tis,
    Comes flying quickly on,
When I must stand the dying test,
    Be lodged in yonder tomb.

3 Dying is not compared
    To the great rising day,
  To see a gracious, smiling God,
    Or frowns of misery.

4 Prepare, prepare me, Lord,
    In ways of righteousness,
  And make Thy Word my only guide,
    My great and sure defense.

5 Dying is going home
    To the afflicted saint—
  Outrides his troubles through the tomb,
    'Tis there his sorrows faint.

6 No more to press him down,
    By howling tempest driven,
  But rise to wear a golden crown
    In the sweet climes of heaven.

7 Where will the wicked go?
    O, what a doleful thought!
  The frowns of God will send below,
    Most surely come to nought.

8 I dare not say the word
    My soul deserved so well;
  Should I have gained the great reward,
    Surely 't would be in hell.

9 But God in mercy sent
    A hope of faith and love,
  Bestowed upon his children here,
    Confirms their joys above.

NO. 201.

1 FAITH! 'tis a precious seed,
 Where'er it is bestowed ;
Takes root within the heavenly mind,
 And scents the Church of God.

2 It is produced by grace,
 A glorious gift of God,
Whereby we look beyond time's space
 Up to our last abode.

3 Faith views Thy goodness, Lord,
 Thy powerful arm to save;
With great delight we view the road
 That leads to joys above.

4 Lord, warm our hearts with grace,
 That we may travel on,
Beholding Thy rich promises
 Through Thy beloved Son.

NO. 202.   C. M.

1 GAIN heaven, I have all things below,
 Without her I have none ;
What is this world, with all her store,
 To that e'erlasting one ?

2 Seek first thy happiness above,
 The Lord, thy righteousness;
And whatsoever things ye need
 Shall charm thy every bliss.

3 What is this world? A fleeting show,
 Wrapt with afflictions here ;
Enticing are her paths below,
 Poison'd with toil and care.

4 While heavenly things move sweetly on,
    With prospects bright and fair,
    Her ports are free for heaven's sons—
    O may I enter there!

NO. 203. C. M.

1 HOW dare I knock at mercy's door,
    Where all my crimes are stored?
    There pointing at me by the score
    Portrays a frowning Lord.

2 My sins—alas! how strong they be!—
    Condemn me down to hell;
    Unless there's mercy shown to me,
    Must with the wicked dwell.

3 I hear them say, "Poor sinner, knock—
    You will admittance gain;"
    But, Oh! how would I there appear,
    With all my sin and pain?

4 His very presence would be hell
    Unto my guilty mind;
    Better for me with devils dwell
    Than stand up there condemned.

5 How can I knock, unless I know
    Where stand the wicket gate?
    Might knock and knock without the door
    Until it is too late.

6 Without some hand should guide me there,
    And plead my sins forgiven,
    My seeking would be all in vain,
    To find the ports of heaven.

7 The Lord must give us courage, hope,
    And bid us rise and go;
  None gain admittance in his court,
    Only whom he foreknew.

3 Whom that he knows he bids them come,
    Nor shall they stay away;
  They plead their cause through his dear Son,
    Who washed their sins away.

9 O may I come, dear Jesus, now?
    Although oppressed with shame,
  I feel the heavens before me bow,
    Through Thy Almighty name.

10 With Thee I have all things below,
    To seek and always gain;
   Admittance will the Lord bestow
    On followers of the Lamb.

NO. 204.   S. M.

1 TOILING and rowing here,
    And gazing for the dawn—
  When will the moments bright appear,
    Shall see my Father's home?

2 No earthly house compare
    In splendor equal His;
  His children are arriving there,
    Sailing through stormy seas.

3 His house, inlaid with gold,
    Without, of cedars fair—
  His children, bought for once, were sold
    In midnight darkness here.

4 Our ransom will appear,
    And land us safe at home;
  Though seas are high, the winds we fear,
    Safely to port we'll come.

5 The seas obey His voice;
    He bids their raging cease,
  Until the children of His choice
    Arrive at home in peace.

NO. 205. L. M.

1 LET sinners rage and men defame—
  Be sure of right, and then proclaim
  Thy God's the God of right and love,
  While none can change His plans above.

2 Nor earth below—they're deeply laid—
  Before the earth or seas were made,
  Jehovah's omnipresent eye
  Has scanned to all eternity.

3 Before the earthen dust was laid,
  His eye was o'er creation stayed;
  Behold His works completely planned,
  His judgment, justice, wisdom manned.

4 While not one jot or tittle erred,
  But e'er fulfilled His mighty word
  Ah! soon shall His archangel soar,
  And swear that time shall be no more.

5 While all the fates of men are sealed
  In the great volume unrevealed—
  When God in judgment shall descend
  And ope the books, who shall defend?

6 Another book shall be revealed—
Through Jesus Christ 'twas ever sealed;
My name may find it written there,
Or shall I sink in keen despair?

7 Shall such a worthless worm as I
Ever succeed to reign on high?
'Tis known to God—be to His praise,
When works of nature's in a blaze.

8 I have a hope he'll own my name;
Acceptance by my Saviour came;
While through His merits here I'll plead—
He's all the wisdom that I need.

9 Yea, should he cast me down to hell,
I must admire His wisdom well;
With eyes too pure to behold sin,
Which my poor soul has wallowed in.

10 But washed in my Redeemer's blood,
Washed out the stains which sin has made—
Through Him the Lord shall view my case,
And save me through His sovereign grace.

NO. 206.   C. M.

1 ILLUSTRIOUS day, when Jesus shines
  Within this soul of mine,
Bid midnight's darkest hours begone,
  And fills with light divine.

2 My soul can mount these lower skies,
  Despite of raging sin;
There will I wipe my weeping eyes,
  When Jesus reigns within.

3 O come, my God and King, proclaim
    My soul forever free
To speak the music of thy name
    In strains of ecstasy.

4 Fain would I sound it out so loud
    That heaven and earth might hear—
The mercies of my God applaud,
    In songs of love and fear.

5 Yea, how exalted here I stand,
    When rays of glory shine;
I long to see our Emanuel's land—
    There shall I call Thee mine.

NO. 207. S. M.

1 DARK was the doleful day
    In which the Saviour died;
Struggling 'twixt life and death was He,
    Our pardon to provide.

2 There standing by the cross,
    His earthly mother wept;
Weep not for me, I've gained the host,
    Enwrapt in Egypt's night.

3 I lay my body down
    For thee, my kindred dear;
The third revolving glorious morn,
    Again I shall appear.

4 No more to bear the scorn
    And scoffs of wicked men;
I shall a nobler name adorn,
    And you shall wear the same.

5 For you I bore the shame—
    Your sins demand a tear;
  Your endless glory to regain,
    This solemn hour appear.

6 I now with sacred awe
    Behold the dreadful scene;
  The holy precepts of that law
    Demand obedience in.

7 I stood condemned in shame,
    Until my God appeared;
  Relief through Him, the sureties name—
    Jesus, thy name revere.

8 May Thy instructions now
    Make my poor soul rejoice,
  And in obedience to Thee bow,
    To honor and embrace.

9 In duty may I own
    Thy name the sinner's friend;
  All other names, dear Lord, dethrone—
    On Thee I will depend.

10 Thy matchless love and power
    Sufficient for my day;
  Encouragements in every hour,
    Persuade me to obey.

11 Rather than not adore
    That God who called me here,
  Let kindred friends keep silence now—
    I must that name revere.

NO. 208. C. M.

1 CHRIST, our High Potentate and King,
    For us endured the cross,
Despised the shame, an offering made,
    That paid the ransom price.

2 Offered to God without one spot,
    Upon the shameful tree;
That memory dear, to those he bought,
    There set the prisoner free.

3 Unlocked the hidden cell of guilt,
    Revealed the man of sin;
Redemption in that blood there spilt,
    Which makes us whole again.

4 He speaks! the sinner soon revives,
    Like one raised from the dead;
Sends forth one ray—he ever lives,
    And will the glory spread.

5 Jesus, our Priest and King, we own
    Thy wisdom and Thy grace;
Now to us make thy blessings known,
    And own us sons of peace.

NO. 209. P. M.

1 BLIND, deaf and dumb below,
    The sons of God appear,
Till Jesus brings to view
    His mercy, love and fear.
Our nature shocked at the dread sight,
To find such massive stores of guilt.

2 The beams of love divine
   Unloosed our fettered chains,
While grace and hope combined
   To ease our troubled pains;
The God of mercy in relief,
Sent us a balm to stop our grief.

3 His Son the tidings brought—
   His name our peace proclaimed;
I have salvation wrought,
   Your pardon to maintain.
O who in silence can now stand,
Who claims relief through Jesus' hand!

4 Rejoice for evermore,
   And spread the news abroad;
There's mercy yet in store—
   Let sinners seek their God;
He is the sinner's only friend,
'Tis he that brought salvation down.

NO. 210.   7s.

1 VAIN are our trifling joys below,
   Composed of sin and shame,
Until more nobler joys we know,
   Comes through our Saviour's name.

2 We claim in nature that we know
   The way to heavenly bliss,
And feel secured in what we do
   Will bring us endless peace.

3 But when a voice from heaven descends,
   With light, and truth and grace,
Our earthly prop begins to bend
   Beneath a dangerous place.

4 No way to flee the dreadful sight,
   For 'tis confined within;
   The law unsafe to make us right—
   We fall condemned in sin.

5 But O, the news revives our hope—
   'Tis sent direct from heaven;
   Jesus appears, the sinner's prop—
   Through Him our sins forgiven.

NO. 211. P. M.

1 HOW lonesome and tiresome
    The hours pass away,
   When Jesus no greeting
    Does send down to me.
   I feel so uneasy,
    So dull and so ill,
   No one can now please me,
    With tastes or with skill.

2 But in one sweet moment,
    When I hear His voice,
   Enough my glad soul
    Cannot but now rejoice.
   In splendor the moments
    Fast gliding away;
   My soul is now lifted
    To that glorious day.

3 Where Jesus in smiles,
    With His pleasure afford,
   Amuse the poor wanderer
    With honors adored.
   Only a foretaste,
    'Tis His pleasure to give,

And draw us by love
In the vale where we live.

4 Ah, soon we will cease
This dark vale to reside,
And arise to the chambers
Of love to abide;]
Where Jesus, the light
Of that thrice glorious day,
With care has prepared
The rich banquet for me.

5 And not for me only,
But for every one
Who looks for his coming
In glory again.
In chariots of fire,
The blest day will soon come;
All glory! All glory!
Our songs will resume.

NO. 212. P. M.

1 COME all who profess,
And are bound for glory,
And listen to the tale
Of my wondrous story.
Long time lived in darkness,
Nor saw my lost state;
Yea, thought my good deeds
Fairly balanced all right.

2 But in one lone hour
Jesus passed by my cot,
Unvailed by his goodness
The state of my heart.

THE WANDERING PILGRIM. 189

The light shone within,
And revealed all my sin—
The works I applauded
Unfit to be seen.

3 A poor, wretched sinner,
For mercy applied,
Although felt unworthy,
My way to decide;
All hope now bewailed me
To right my lost case,
Until I heard of one
That could save me by grace.

3 I could not see how
With the Word that would do,
For all I had read
Did condemn me to woe;
But when all things proved
A failure to me,
I stood there resolved
To try the remedy.

5 But lost and undone,
I could not find the way;
Completely o'erwhelmed,
To save could not be.
In darkness and grief,
I gave up in despair;
While mercy I plead,
For the Lord to forbear.

6 In calmness of night,
There sprang joy to my soul,
In streams of delight,
I felt every whit whole;

The voice of free grace
Was to me there applied,
Through the wounds of my Jesus,
His hands and His side.

7 My guilt all removed,
And my tongue praising God,
With joy unsurpassed,
For an angel to 'plaud;
My feelings couldn't hide,
The display that I spied,
The smiles of my Saviour,
And Him crucified.

8 Encouraged with hope
To believe on his name,
And that He has died
My poor soul to redeem;
To love and obey
Was His blessed command,
And that with his children
I've taken my stand.

9 Though foes much oppress,
And try to frighten me,
And fears will suggest,
Hadn't I better delay?
I press onward where
Duty calls me to go,
Although much embarrassed
In darkness and woe.

10 These storms I'll outride,
For the day's hastening on—
The landmarks all point
To Emanuel's land.

He bids me not fear,
For foes can't molest;
Yea, soon he'll appear,
And receive me at rest.

NO. 213. P. M.

1 AFFLICTED, despised,
Rejected to stand,
With cedars in this
Professed Christian land;
They're tall in esteem,
And applauded and gay,
With plenty of means
To reach well on their way.

2 In means I have none
To convey me along,
But live on the mercy,
The God of my song,
Who sees to my wants,
And supplies what I need,
And bids me to follow
My guide is His Word.

3 To error aloof
Is the word of command,
And stand for the truth,
Though your foes shall condemn;
I'll guide thee, direct thee,
Thy pathway to find,
While foes and all fears
Shall be left to the wind.

4 Yea, galleys with oars
Shall come puffing along,

And look with defiance
  On the nymphs of your song;
They'll teach grace is free
  For you and for me;
But unless we comply
  The Saviour will deny.

5 And when we have sought,
  Must continue the rout,
Comply with the Gospel,
  And work your way out;
Work out your salvation,
  Your souls to adorn;
Then Jesus will own you
  That great noted morn.

6 The sinner may come
  Whenever he may choose—
Comply with the Gospel,
  And never refuse.
But, Oh! my affliction
  Right here now begins;
Instead of my choosing,
  The Saviour proclaims:

7 "I've loved thee—I died
  Thy poor soul to provide
A ransom from sin,
  And thy errors to chide;
My grace is sufficient
  To bring your supplies;
Your wants are my care,
  And your toil is my praise.

8 I wrought your salvation
  Upon Calvary's tree;

Yea, died and arose,
   To set your poor soul free.
I hold you, preserve you,
   And keep from all harm,
And only require you
   My name to adorn.

9 Show forth to the world
   Your zeal and your love,
For men to acknowledge
   Your'e taught from above.
Although they'll reject
   And despise you below,
Thy namesake is what
   Makes their anger to grow.

10 Press forward! I'll never
   Forsake or leave thee;
Thy steps I'll direct,
   And will teach what to say;
The end of thy journey
   I will receive thee,
Where foes and all fears
   Will vanish away.

11 In presence of angels
   To shout and adore
Thy God and thy Saviour,
   In triumphs e'er more.
Thy song and thy praise,
   Forever will be,
The God that did die,
   And arose to save thee.

NO. 214. P. M.

1 JESUS is the name adored
  By the honored sons of God;
  In his treasures are there stored
  All their medicine and food:
      Like a river
  Ever flows from Thee, O Lord!

2 'Mid creation's sounding fame,
  What are titles to Thy name?
  A few days and life is o'er,
  While Thee, ever to adore,
      None to sever,
  None to chase our souls away.

3 Yea, in Jesus I have rest.
  In his name I'm ever blest;
  While the world my wanderings chide,
  Yea, my faults I cannot hide.
      Cheerful giver!
  May I shelter by thy side.

4 When the storm of life is o'er,
  Land above on Canaan shore,
  Where my God and friend adore,
  There in triumph evermore;
      Bound with Jesus,
  In celestial worlds to soar.

NO. 215. P. M.

1 VAIN delusive world, adieu,
    You have no charms for me;
  Pleasures are mere toys to know
    That's formed of vanity.

Fading with the morning sun,
Prospectus fair but never won,
Leave an aching heart to know
The source where sorrows flow.

2 Methinks I see a better day,
   Where joys forever flow,
Wrapt in songs of ecstacy;
   Aye, none but pilgrims know.
Give me, Lord, a taste below
To seek where Thy rich treasures grow,
There to bask this soul of mine
In joys of love divine.

3 Yea, I would here follow Thee,
   Incline me, Lord, to go;
Leave this earthly vanity
   For other ones to know.
Let me be by grace upheld,
Thy name my only hope and shield;
Follow where my duty leads,
Thy glorious name to spread.

4 Soon these anxions cares and toil
   Will cease thy soul to grieve,
Join the nobler host on high,
   Thy soul shall be relieved.
There, in one most glorious strain,
Sing of Jesus' wondrous fame;
Yea, my song shall ever be,
The Lamb that bled for me.

NO. 216.   P. M.

1 COME, O my friends, remember,
   What Jesus done for you;

Ah, silent was thy danger,
　Fast rolling on to view.
He made the roving monster
　Fast in weighty chains,
While all our sad disaster
　Combined his dying pains.

2 Released from every burden,
　Our sins the massive load;
Yea, hid beyond the Jordan,
　The stain of Adam's blood.
Persuaded by His calling,
　We are the sons of God,
Secured from ever falling,
　Through His most precious blood.

3 'Tis finished, cried the Saviour,
　Upon the accursed tree,
And by obedience tender
　His life for you and me;
Yea, by His spirit calls us,
　Our every burden leave,
Follow the pattern gave us
　Of faith and hope and love.

4 Be not ashamed to own me
　Before a frowning race.
My life a ransom gave thee,
　To bring thee home in peace.
And when the battle's over,
　The rage of sin and strife,
I shall thy bodies cover
　With an immortal life.

NO. 217. P. M.

1 O, YE sinners in the tomb,
   Pointing where Moses lay,
   Yea, his grave ye cannot find,
   Though seeking night and day.
   O'er the mountain's top to vie,
   Canaan's land before you die.
   In the vale's the crossing ground,
   Jesus the stream must sound.

2 Looking on beyond for help,
   Through precepts of the law,
   Yea, where all our fathers slept,
   A nobler day to view.
   Touch ye not the mountain's strand,
   For it is a burning land;
   It will kill the sinner dead
   When on the mount he tread.

3 Jesus will the soul revive
   Seeking the law is killed;
   Raise him up in peace to live
   Where heavenly blessings filled.
   Streams of mercy every hour
   Flowing from His heavenly power,
   Send forth joy and love and peace,
   Strengthened by every grace.

4 Come, poor sinner, now is need,
   In Jesus put your trust,
   'Tis by Him your souls are freed,
   Who finds out they are lost.
   Seek Him in His courts to-day,
   Troubles may attend delay,
   Trust in Him, He ne'er will wrong,
   He is the Christian song.

NO. 218. P. M.

1 SHOULD I please with pleasant speech
Worldlings minds where e'er I preach,
Proof sufficient something wrong,
Should the world applaud my song.
Nature claims to know the way,
Leading into endless day;
Jesus says nature is blind,
And the heavenly path can't find.

2 Jesus sends His spirit down,
Quickening both the deaf and dumb,
Giving sight unto the blind,
Through His name their wisdom find
A way they had ne'er sought;
Taken by a backward route,
Crossed poor nature's knowing path,
Closed his mouth, appeased his wrath.

3 Should I seek the world's applause,
'Twould not be my master's cause;
Yea, the word must give offense
If its preached in Scripture sense.
Jesus will His own provide,
Through the furnace shall be tried;
Seek the honors of His name,
Leave their own from whence it came.

NO. 219. S. M.

1 COME, heavenly tongues, and swell
    The powers of Jesus' grace—
The glories of that beauty tell,
    When you did see His face.

2 In robes of beauty shine,
   His wisdom and His skill,
To clothe withal His favorite name,
   Who still on earth does dwell.

3 Soon shall they soar above,
   His graces to describe,
There sing fore'er that God is love,
   With all the holy tribe.

NO. 220. 7s.

1 HEAVENLY joy await the saints,
   Bound in bonds of lasting love;
He who knows their every want,
   Shall their peace provide above.

2 In ecstatic strains they'll sing,
   Jesus, Advocate and Head;
He's their Saviour, God and King—
   Salvation the theme adored.

3 Joined by all the heavenly host,
   To praise the Father, Holy Ghost,
And the Son, as three in one,
   Round one glorious, shineing throne.

NO. 221. C. M.

1 JESUS! Thy loving name adored
   By heavenly tongues below,
They shall declare Thy honors, Lord,
   Thy grace and virtue too.

2 Thy loving name revives our hope
   For better things above;
The music breaks the swelling note,
   And scents our joys with love.

3 Keep silent now—the rocks would burst,
　To speak God's matchless praise,
While heavenly tongues on earth would thirst
　In search of nobler days.

4 Prisons and chains cannot confine
　The beauties of that name,
But what the crystal gem will shine
　Throughout the world the same.

NO. 222.　　　　P. M.

1 THE truth it is mighty,
　　And it will prevail;
　Though friends will oppose,
　　And my foes shall assail,
　The Word I must preach,
　　And my Jesus declare,
　The way and the truth
　　That upholds Zion here.

2 He guides me, defends me,
　　While dwelling below—
　In mercy compels me
　　His merits to show.
　To obey's my delight—
　　May I faithfully prove,
　With expressions of light,
　　'Tis the truth that I love.

3 In the vale, on the mountain,
　　The storm I fear not,
　The truth to proclaim;
　　Yea, I feel 'tis my lot,
　The worth of my Saviour
　　Poor sinners to tell.
　His love in their favor
　　Will save them from hell.

4 Although they are tossed
    By storms of distress,
  Nothing shall come cross them
    He cannot suppress.
  His truth is their guide,
    And His name is their song;
  Their need will provide,
    As they journey along.

5 Ay! soon we shall leave
    For a more healthful clime.
  Where foes can't assail,
    And our sun ever shine.
  Unceasing our song,
    While our joys are divine;
  The Host be adored
    Through Jesus' name.

NO. 223.   C. M.

1 COME, follow me, my Master cries,
    I'll make you fishermen,
  The net I've cast, my hands have made,
    I'll bring it safe to land.

2 The good and bad the net will vie,
    My glory draws them in,
  Some for the food, yea, some to see
    The miracles performed.

3 The good receive, the bad refuse,
    Your judgment must display
  To judge 'twixt Gentiles and the Jews,
    Your Master to obey.

4 My children will compose the good,
    You'll tell them by their voice,

The warbling of their swelling notes
   Will tremble and rejoice.

5 They'll tell you what ensnared them in
   The Gospel's seeking net;
To flee the rages of their sin,
   Their tender passions caught.

6 The task is great, your foes are strong,
   Will seek your overthrow,
My grace sufficient shall supply
   You all the journey through.

7 'Midst all the storms of envy here,
   Not one shall ever harm;
And when your work on earth is done,
   I'll bring you joyful home.

8 The welcome news shall there receive,
   Ye faithful servant come,
Enter the joys thy Lord's prepared,
   With all the honors won.

NO. 224.   S. M.

1 IT doth not yet appear,
   But confidence bestowed
By Him who rules our every fear,
   We shall be like our Lord.

2 Beyond one shadowing doubt,
   The people of our choice,
Shall find that kingdom they have sought,
   With Jesus to rejoice.

3 Though worms devour this flesh,
   And nature must decay;
The Lord His sons will clothe afresh
   In one eternal day.

4 Though conflicts doth entwine,
   Around their hidden way,
  Their God provides their joys divine
   And makes their darkness day.

5 He is our all below
   And ours above the sky;
  To cross the vale we all must go,
   Our joys are fixed on high.

6 Impatiently we stand,
   Not to be unclothed here,
  But clothed upon by Jesus' hand,
   His expressed image bear.

NO. 225. 7s.

1 LORD, revive my lingering hope,
   For I feel so dry and dull;
  Make me feel that grace I need—
   Are not all Thy treasures full?

2 If I am, why should I feel
   Cold and lifeless to Thy cause?
  Come and break this heart of steel,
   Fill with grace Thy name to 'plause.

3 Can a Christian ever be
   Quite so trifling as I am?
  Ever through my life I see
   Thy rich mercy still the same.

4 O, so prone to wander here,
   Prone to leave the God I love;
  Lord, to me wilt Thou appear?
   Raise my willing thoughts above.

5 Drink the flowing streams of love,
   Filled with hope and faith and zeal,
Till I reach Thy joys above,
   No more these cold hours to feel.

6 There where darkness ne'er affright,
   Wandering thoughts no more to stray,
There to drink with sweet delight
   The rich pleasures of that day.

NO. 226.   C. M.

1 WHEN I look back my life to read,
   Thy mercies I survey,
Thou wondrous, universal God,
   Who called me here below—

2 Through every step of joy or woe,
   I trace Thy matchless hand,
Converting all the ways I go,
   To meet Thy great command.

3 I rest secure in Thy embrace,
   Though troubles face me here;
I still will trust Thy sovereign grace
   To guide my feet from fear.

4 And when the day of storm is o'er,
   Life's journey here is run,
I shall arise to mount the shore
   Where troubles never come.

5 There see the work of God complete,
   Without a vail between—
There bow low at my Saviour's feet,
   My Advocate and King!

6 Jesus, when shall that day appear,
  And all Thine armies shine,
Without one cloud to interfere?—
  The glory shall be Thine.

NO. 227.   S. M.

1 WHY was it Adam fell?
  Why did he stoop so low?
His progeny in misery hurl,
  Far in the depths of woe!

2 Why is it fishes rove,
  Far in the mighty sea,
There seek the food on which they live,
  With great delight and glee?

3 Why is it birds do fly
  High in the open air,
Guided by nature's hand to spy
  Their daily rations there?

4 Why is it Christians love
  To cheer the mercy seat,
And seek their food on joys above,
  Low at their Saviour's feet?

5 The whole I'll answer here—
  One line shall bear the dent;
And why? Because it does appear
  To be their element.

6 Yea, God has formed us so,
  His nature's work to adorn;
Out of the earth he made us grow
  Our nature and our form—

7 Except the Christian mind,
    Which grows in heavenly clime,
    Prepared by God and planted here,
    For nobler joys divine.

8 The fishes for the sea,
    The winged fowls to fly,
    The mystery of the whole appear,
    The man of vanity.

9 Man formed out of the earth,
    No higher joys can span,
    Until he does receive the birth
    Of God, called the new man.

10 This earthly house the same,
    Under subjections driven,
    Growing until his change shall come
    For nobler joys in heaven.

NO. 228. 7s.

1 FIRST of all, my friends, I say,
    Seek the heavenly kingdom,
  There to court thine earthly stay,
    There to enjoy thy soul's freedom.

2 Seek the Lord, His righteousness—
    He's the Christian's only guide;
  For thine earthly happiness,
    From His bounties shall provide.

3 Thy delay will bring thee fears,
    Lonesome, backward life to rove,
  Shall regret in riper years,
    Did not build thy joys above.

4 Come now, while your hearts are warm.
   Cares and toils have not begun ;
   Yea, the host now bids you come—
   See, their doors are open flung.

5 Welcome bids from every star,
   Planted by our Father's hand,
   Who are brought from nations far,
   In the kingdom meekly shine.

6 Grace and virtue shall adorn
   Our Father's kingdom here,
   Formed for all the noble sons
   In his image to appear.

7 When the work of grace is done,
   And the Lord our spirits vie,
   Shall a nobler house adorn,
   Far above the lurid sky.

NO. 229.   P. M.

1 I WILL advance an idea
   Before I leave the sod ;
   The angels are the servants
   That speak the sacred word,
   Divide the sinners from the saints,
   Proclaiming what their Master wants.
      Offense drives off the ill,
      While Christians get their fill.

2 Jesus is the great Sower
   That sends the Word broadcast;
   To angels gave he power
   To reap the great harvest.
   Behold them wield the glittering sword,
   Confirmed by heaven's attending word.

The chaff will flee away,
While fruit shall gathered be.

3 Some think the angel teacher
   Should speak in pleasant smile,
To be a faithful preacher
   Should not offend the vile;
To preach the Word must cross their track,
Uphold the cause for Jesus' sake;
   Yea, men nor devils fear,
   While they His name declare.

4 The Word must cross our nature,
   Proclaimed by grace divine;
The angels are the reapers,
   The tares in bundles bind;
Their glist'ning sickles are so sharp,
They'll cut exactly to the mark,
   Dividing all offenders
   Who are such pretenders.

5 The world, the harvest's on us—
   Behold the angels now,
Whose glittering swords around us
   Are steel of finest show;
And in the kingdom shall condemn
The state of those that shall offend;
   There shall the righteous shine
   Bright as the noon-day sun.

6 These words may we consider,
   To stand or fall I know;
They do my mind bewilder—
   Shall I be left to grow?
Shall I among the righteous shine,
This poor, bewildered soul of mine?
   Not scarce one leaf can show,
   While dwelling here below.

NO. 230.

1 DRESSED, uniformed, the soldiers wear
   All of one tinted shade—
   Not made upon their orders here,
   But by their Captain drawed.

2 The Christian soldier wears withal
   A robe of equal dress,
   Wrought out by Jesus' hand, and shall
   Complete their righteousness.

3 Their coats of armor, and, yea, more,
   Their helmet and their shield,
   The Captain shall His men adore,
   And teach them not to yield.

4 Though struggling in the conflict here,
   His love does constant cheer;
   Amidst the trials they endure,
   He bids them never fear.

5 Ay! soon their warfare will be o'er,
   They shall the vict'ry don;
   The lambs shall their names adore,
   Through God's eternal Son.

6 They shall arise to nobler fields,
   Where war is never heard;
   The glory of their songs shall yield
   Their banners to the Lord.

NO. 231.

1 A NOBLEMAN made a great feast,
   And opened doors out wide,
   When to behold the invited guest
   His soul with horror vied.

2 "I should have watched," said he, "with care;
   My foes are in the house;
   They haunt my liberty to share;
   With them I can't rejoice."

3 The servants in their welcome haste
   Did not observe with care,
   And gathered to the rich repast
   Unwelcome ones e'en there.

4 The king was wrath, for one without
   A wedding garment on,
   He bade his servants bind him there,
   And cast him out anon.

5 In like manner, the Church in glee,
   Too anxious here to fill,
   Invites her foes to come and see,
   And bend to Zion's will.

6 When they our liberty have spied,
   Unto their own will go;
   But not without our cause have tried
   To melt us down in woe.

7 With care the servant here should seek
   The contrite heart to know,
   And shun the feet of those who make
   A great and flowery show.

8 Not many wise or noble here
   Our Heavenly Father calls;
   But from those of a humble peer,
   That seeks to do his will.

NO. 232. S. M.

1 WHAT worthless worms are we!
   Born of the earth at first,

And soon must to the earth return,
There drop this dying flesh.

2 But God will soon revive
And clothe our forms afresh,
E'er in His kingdom shall we live,
With an immortal dress.

3 Wrought out by Jesus' hands,
On Calv'ry's bloody cross
He died to free our dreadful bonds,
And yet sustained no loss.

4 And we who look for Him,
Shall He again appear,
Beyond the powers of death and sin,
Yea, man nor devil's fear.

5 Ascend the lofty skies,
Ye ransomed host of God ;
The welcome day shall soon arise,
A day of sweet record.

6 The swelling of our songs
Will make the heavens ring ;
Jesus has tuned our voices here
To chant the notes we'll sing.

NO. 233. P. M.

1 JESUS, with all His servants,
In every age has been ;
He's led them through the furnace,
Yea, in the lion's den ;
Yea, in the stocks they have rejoiced
To hear their Heavenly Master's voice,
To see the dead arise,
And seek with weeping eyes.

2 Behold! the astonished jailer
    Awoke, awhile dismayed,
But found the prisoners in there,
    Though all the doors unbarred,
Come trembling in and falling down,
Arose and washed the gushing wounds
    Of Paul and Silas too,
    Crying, "What shall I do?"

3 They said, "Believe on Jesus,
    And do thyself no harm;
He is the one that freed us
    From malady and sin;
He and His household did arise,
That self-same hour, and was baptized,
    Rejoicing in their word,
    As angels from the Lord.

O! may thy servants pray thee,
    Yet glorious days to wand;
Seek out the weeping Marys,
    Who are for Zion bound;
And more than all the Lydias find,
To seek their want of need to bind,
    While dwelling here below,
    Midst every sin and woe.

5 The crown is still before them,
    Their King they will applaud;
The Church should well adore them
    As servants of the Lord;
Yea, soon their labor will be done,
The harvest reapt, the laurels won,
    And they the crown receive,
    E'er with their King to live.

NO. 234.　　C. M.

1 YEA! blessed day, when first the Lord
　Inspired my heart with zeal
　To claim the blessings in thy word
　That leads to Zion's hill.

2 My sins erased, how far unknown
　To my poor mortal eyes;
　While grace and mercy to me shown
　In beams from heavenly skies.

3 My joy could not be here surpassed
　By nature's fleeting rays,
　To be invited there a guest,
　There sing my Saviour's praise.

4 One day, dear Lord, within Thy court,
　Is worth ten thousand here;
　The blissful thought! my name is wrote,
　E'en in Thy books appear.

NO. 235.　　C. M.

1 O SOLEMN day! my heart aspire
　To reach thy blissful rays;
　Could I but see the heavenly fire,
　'Twould make my soul to blaze.

2 I would o'er mount these trials here,
　In songs of sweet delight—
　With willing footsteps trace the way
　That leads to heaven's height.

3 But I am bound in fettered chains,
　One blissful ray can't see;
　Dear Lord! O come, undo my reins
　And set the prisoner free.

NO. 236.   S. M.

1 JESUS! Thy charming name!
   What music does enclose!
 Combined within thy glorious fame,
   For those in Thee were chose.

2 Chosen of God, and dear
   To him the sacred name;
 His mercy lent a list'ning ear,
   When all their help was gone.

3 Jesus, the son of God,
   Their pardon to maintain,
 Poured out His precious, crimson blood,
   To stay their sin and shame.

4 The debt He freely paid—
   Yea, all their sorrows bore;
 His love's sufficient for their aid
   Were they ten thousand more.

5 O, may I ever find
   My name recorded there,
 My peace and pardon both entwined,
   Amongst his generous care.

NO. 237.   P. M.

1 JESUS wept! What solemn feeling
   These few words to us portray!
 O may we, with voices heeding,
   Think of Jesus here to-day,
     Jesus weeping!
 Were those briny tears for me?

2 Jesus wept! What lonely feeling!
  Cannot shed one tear for him!
'Twas for love a kindred meaning;
  Could I read the sentence mine!
    Glory shining
  Through those heavenly tears divine.

3 Jesus wept! O, careless sinner!
  Were those tears for you and me?
Dare we not to claim the banner,
  With a solemn thought to-day?
    Sleeping sinner!
  Must the mighty voice obey.

4 Jesus wept! The Jews did chide him;
  How could He love Lazarus so?
Surely there is nothing lacking—
  Roll the mighty stone away!
    Sleeping Lazarus!
  Yea, the mighty God calls forth.

5 Yea! behold! he was but sleeping,
  Who was numbered with the dead,
Coming forth at Jesus' speaking!
  O, what power was there portrayed!
    Come we praying,
  Wilt Thou raise our dying head?

6 Raise to Thine eternal glory,
  There to reign with Thee, our Lord,
Chiming forth the endless story,
  Jesus can restore the dead!
    Endless pleasure!
  We will see no weeping there.

NO. 238. 8s, 7s, 4s.

1 ENDLESS pleasures now are chiming
 Round our Father's shining throne;
 Lo! the Church is still arriving—
 Jesus there will call his own.
  Shall I welcome
 Hear His voice my name proclaim?

2 Shall I sing, that name adorning,
 Pleading there in my behalf?
 When I was enwrapt in mourning,
 And no path to guide one self,
  Jesus pleading,
 Pleading there in my behalf.

3 May I hear Thee greet with pleasure—
 "Come, thou loved one of the Lord,
 Come thou here, receive thy treasure,
 Prepared for the sons of God.
  Endless treasure
 At His own right is stored.

NO. 239. C. M.

1 HOW should I come before the Lord,
  There claim a rightful home?
 Yea, should I plead through Jesus' name,
  Or something I have done?

2 Were there conditions left for me
  To reach the Gospel plea?
 Or must I plead salvation's free
  For poor and worthless me?

THE WANDERING PILGRIM. 217

3 To ask my bosom, soon will tell
    My great delight and glee,
'Twas on the road that leads to hell,
    When Jesus spoke to me.

4 My feet fast sticking in the mire,
    He opened mine eyes to see;
I saw my case was one of dire
    In endless misery.

5 Jesus the pleasing news revealed,
    And raised me from the pit—
Showed me that my salvation's free,
    I've paid the ransom debt.

6 Come, follow me, my love to show—
    Adorn thy God and King;
This is thy duty here below,
    To spread thy Saviour's name.

7 Conditions now I do require,
    If ye would peace enjoy;
Put on my yoke, the cross to bear,
    And follow after me.

8 The way I've marked for thee to go,
    'Twill lead to joys on high;
But should thou miss the path below,
    'Twill bring much sorrow nigh.

9 Dear Lord! I will now try to run
    In Thy delightful way;
May I all other ways e'er shun,
    That leads the soul astray.

NO. 240. C. M.

1 NOW let these words suffice to know
   That I am still alive,
Though I have been, they thought so low,
   So very near my grave.

2 The Lord in mercy has appeared
   To be my chief delight;
Yea, raised up my poor drooping head,
   And taught me how to write.

3 Enclosed a golden pen withal,
   Angels to guide my hand,
To go where treasures, rich and full,
   In my Emanuel's land.

4 This world to me is but a show,
   Fast gliding on its way,
Fulfilling God's designs below,
   As time rolls on the day.

5 He has designs for me to work,
   Yea, I couldn't think it so;
I did out of my duty lurk,
   Until He brought me low.

6 With promises from time to time,
   I have the cross foreborne,
Till now He has my lot entwined—
   I can't but use my pen.

7 On crutches I am hobbling long,
   Yea, worse; within my mind
Can't think of one good thankful song
   To applaud my God and King.

8 The Lord both kills and makes alive,
　　Yea, plants His heavenly name;
　His spirit will not always strive
　　With man to tell His fame.

9 He brings us low and raises up
　　For means to us unknown,
　His purposes are deep indeed,
　　Unfolding from His throne.

10 The beggar sunk in poverty
　　Beholds His mighty power,
　Raise up with men of high degree,
　　Yea makes a millionaire.

11 The same where He desires to place
　　His wisdom and His love,
　Conveys to us His stores of grace,
　　Drawn from the heights above.

12 His treasuries are forever sealed,
　　None but His power unlocks;
　He gives poor mortals here to feel
　　The glory of His works.

13 Could I but have one morsel here,
　　How would my soul rejoice;
　Yea, in His secret court appear
　　To hear the heavenly voice.

14 But dry and dull my seasons are,
　　O, would the Lord inspire
　My soul to have one blessing here,
　　E'en from the sacred choir.

15 Reach down, reach down, Almighty God,
　　Thine arm of grace, and cause
　My soul encouraged by Thy word,
　　To choose Thy wholesome laws.

16 The Chaldeans dwell here in our midst,
    Who seek the Lord by art;
   They claim His power and still insist
    'Tis they who do the work.

17 They're seeking night and day, and fall
    On whom they can devour,
   And say, we must begin withal
    To reach the heavenly bower.

18 Ah, sure enough, but how can we
    Unless some one should guide,
   And teach us lessons from that book,
    Yea, all our sorrows hide.

19 If we would seek the Holy Law,
    It kills in every word,
   But grace designs that we should draw
    Our blessings from the Lord.

20 Therefore the Lord must make the way,
    First kill the creature will,
   Then teach us how we must obey
    While grace inspires our zeal.

21 Come then what will, when Jesus speaks
    No power can stay the force,
   When once the heart of steel he breaks
    And melts by sovereign grace.

22 The good Samaritan indeed
    Pours in the oil and wine,
   And by his charities supplied
    We draw from time to time.

23 And when our wounds are healed, yea, more,
    Will take us home to rest;
   There on that sweet and blissful shore
    Where foes no more molest.

24 O, what a happy day indeed,
    When Zion's sons get home,
From foes and sin and wounds are freed,
    There meet around the throne.

24 There sing the song on earth begun
    'Midst sin and sorrow driven,
Beyond the tune of angels formed,
    It is the joys of heaven.

NO. 241.   7s.

1 HEAVENLY Father, come and reign
    In this wandering heart of mine,
My poor soul would ever deign
    To engage Thy cause divine.
Sweetest pleasure, heavenly bliss,
Flows from Thy rich promises.

2 Should I ever from Thee stray,
    Gently will Thy hand correct;
My delight 'tis to obey,
    Guide my willing footsteps right,
May I soon the blessing win,
Freed from sorrow, care and sin.

3 Heavenly prospects cheer mine eyes,
    Glad the solemn day appear.
Come, unvail the lower skies,
    Welcome winged angels bear.
There where God my Saviour reigns,
There where I'll be freed from pains.

NO. 242.   C. M.

1 HOW sweet the blissful hour when first
   I felt my sins forgiven;
 What streams of mercy quenched my thirst
   And sealed my hope for heaven.

2 I ran the blissful road with joy,
   And looked the promise o'er,
 Without thought my soul to annoy,
   I scanned the heavenly shore.

3 Alas, but soon some clouds withal
   Misted my heavenly sky;
 My brightened hope yea soon did fall,
   While sorrows passed me by.

4 But soon the clouds passed over me,
   The sun again did shine
 With that delightful brilliancy
   As when I first began.

5 From doubts and fears I've traveled on
   Through sorrows deep and wide;
 By faith they drive me to that boon
   Where all my fears subside.

6 I can but trust in that dear name
   Where all my hope is stayed;
 Yea, soon to reach the heavenly plain
   No more to feel dismayed.

7 No more to close the parting hand
   Of kindred friends most dear,
 But join in that celestial land
   Where all my hopes appear.

NO. 243. 7s.

CHRISTMAS.

1 SHALL the Lord again appear
   'Midst our sin and shame and fear;
   Shall he suffer on the cross,
   There to purge our guilt and dross.

2 Yea, He shall again appear,
   But not He to suffer here.
   In the splendor of His ire,
   To behold shall I be there.

3 Shall He call my worthless name,
   Raise me to a state of fame;
   Or shall I my just reward
   Receive from Thy hands, O Lord.

4 Teach me, Lord, Thy name to adore;
   O, for grace to love Thee more;
   In my last expiring breath,
   Thy delight to sing in death.

NO. 244. S. M.

1 WEARY and sore distressed
   I find myself this morn,
   Languid with fears and sin oppressed
   I feel somewhat forlorn.

2 Could I but have one glimpse
   Of Thee, my Saviour, God,
   To chase away the darksome hours
   And lean upon Thy word.

3 But I am stumbling here
    'Midst sin and sorrow driven,
  Without one ray to cheer me on
    To find the port of heaven.

4 Grant me, O Lord of love,
    One glimmering ray of Thee,
  Raise my affections high above
    The kings of vanity.

5 And when that day appear
    That brings the soul release,
  May I but worship in Thy fear,
    Consoled with love and peace.

NO. 245.   C. M.

1 COME children of the heavenly king,
    Thy Saviour's name adore,
  Together let us sweetly sing,
    Repeat His mercy o'er.

2 His kindness in our paths He strewed
    When we were sinking down,
  Beneath our sins, a massive load,
    Our worthless name He owned.

3 Instead of wrath, which we deserved,
    From His Almighty name,
  His grace and mercy we received
    With love to greet the same.

4 O, let us ever spread that name
    O'er earth's remotest bounds,
  Tell the poor sinners, halt and lame,
    There's balm to heal their wounds.

THE WANDERING PILGRIM. 225

5 'Tis in the Saviour's noble worth
   His grace is rich and free,
And sinners bound in chains and death
   Through Him released will be.

NO. 246.   P. M.

1 I AM weary of life's journey,
   Through weals and woes,
Oppressed with dullness,
   Affliction and foes.
My happiness faints,
   And I'm pressed down with grief,
No comfort in store
   To subdue unbelief.

2 Dear Lord, rescue darkness
   And give me some light;
I'd rest in the promise,
   Were sure all was right;
But I feel distressed
   In sin and in shame,
And yet can't account,
   No one but self to blame.

3 O, could I but live
   As my duty require,
I'd leave all my fears
   For my foes to admire,
And press for that mark
   Centered far 'bove the skies,
Illumined by God,
   And transcribed for the wise.

4 But my best thoughts are
   Mixed with sin and with shame,

And e'er I attempt
   To speak in Jesus' name,
I fail the oblation
   To bring to His praise,
While seeming distress
   Will destroy the sweet lays.

5 Aught may my poor soul
   Ever bring on the cause;
Dear Lord keep me from
   Ever breaking Thy laws.
To sustain 'Tis delight
   Could I do it aright;
And Thy name glorified,
   And approved in Thy sight.

6 My remnant of days
   May I spend in Thy praise,
And glorify Thee
   As the song of my praise.
And when days and years
   Here allotted are o'er,
Sing praise in perfection
   To Thee on that shore.

7 Where sorrow and darkness
   Shall no more oppress,
Complete in Thy glory
   My robe and my dress,
Where all Thy dear children
   In time shall arrive,
And shout o'er the victory
   Through Thee they've received.

8 In pleasures of love
   And delight shall we rove,

And echo the chorus
Of Jesus above.
Innumerable years
Still the song shall resound;
Yea, cheerful and sweet
As when it first begun.

NO. 247. C. M.

1 DELIGHTFUL theme! when I can see
My Saviour's smiling face,
'Tis then I'll bid farewell to fear
Of every shape and size.

2 Though sin and sorrow should engage
To sink me down to hell,
When Jesus smiles let Satan rage,
And all his malice hurl.

3 One single shaft can ever hit,
Nor harm me here below,
Unless my Saviour God sees fit
To sink me down in woe.

4 Although I fall, I'll trust His grace
Will raise me up again,
Secure my hope will ever last,
And in His kingdom reign.

NO. 248. P. M.

1 WHEN shall I see my Saviour's face,
And in His lovely bosom rest,
To sing redeeming love—
There with the people of His choice
Proclaim the Saviour's pard'ning voice
In yonder courts above?

2 No more annoyed with sin and fear—
No more oppressed with sorrow here—
  But sing of sins forgiven.
O, what a happy day 'twill be!
O'er death we'll claim the victory,
  The entrance to that heaven.

3 On angel's wings we'll soar away
To the bright world of endless day,
  Clapping our hands for joy;
No more despised, no more oppressed,
But with the Saviour ever blest
  To all eternity!

NO. 249.

1 WHAT charming words from Jesus flow
To the poor soul sunk down in woe,
Whose sins, like mountains, o'er him rise,
And hides his mansion in the skies.

2 When Jesus speaks, says "lovest thou me,"
The soul is filled with heavenly glee,
While sin and darkness disappear,
And loving music quells his fear.

3 O, happy souls, whom Jesus loves,
And gives a sight of fields above,
Inspired to sing their sins are freed
Through Jesus Christ their Sovereign Head.

4 O, could I sing his love and power,
And raised within that heavenly bower,
Where none but Jesus would I know,
Where ought but faith and mercy grow.

5 But lo! my mind is grov'ling here,
   Midst sin and darkness, doubts and fear,
   With but a glimmering hope quite small,
   That if a saint, the least of all.

6 But Jesus, who makes these hopes grow,
   O, condescend to let me know,
   Are all my sins on earth forgiven?
   Yea, is my hope sealed up in heaven?

NO. 250. P. M.

1 THE voice of the turtle
   Is heard in our land;
   The winter is o'er,
   And the summer's at hand.
   Come, kindred and friends,
   Let us sing songs of peace,
   Since Jesus has spread·
   His bright rays o'er the place.

2 The winter nigh froze
   Us poor mortals to death,
   And turned friends to foes,
   Despised, bereft;
   But Jesus has smiled,
   And the storm is quite o'er,
   O, may we in triumph
   His name to adore.

3 Inviting young converts
   To tell of His grace
   That freed them of sin,
   And restored to peace,
   Confirmed by the goodness
   Of Jesus their King,

Who loosed their tongues,
  And inspired them to sing.

4 Come, old pilgrims, who
    Have stood long through the storm
  Of sin and derision,
    Afflicted, cast down,
  Arise from thy slumbers,
    Thy God to adorn,
  And rejoice in the day
    Thy salvation begun.

5 Encourage young converts
    Their Master to own,
  By obeying the precepts
    To them He's made known;
  To honor, adore,
    The blest name to us given,
  Till God shall delight
    To remove us to heaven.

NO. 251. S. M.

1 COME, sing to me of heaven,
    Of wisdom, truth, and grace;
  Dear Jesus! may I sing forgiven
    Of all my trespasses?

2 O, sing to me that name,
    Condensed of joy and love,
  And melt this heart into a flame
    Of happiness above.

3 Then shall I love that name
    That called me here below;
  While all my songs shall be the fame
    That Jesus saves from woe.

4 Sing on, ye ransomed! now
   Thy King forever reigns;
   'Tis He that teaches thee to know
   Through Him forgiveness comes.

NO. 252. C. M.

1 SALVATION sent to dying men,
   By Jesus' hands 'tis given;
   By faith receives the promise, when
   Our hope ascends to heaven.

2 It heals the wounds of sin and death,
   And changes every ill—
   Gives us new life, new ways, new breath,
   To run toward Zion's hill.

3 It guards us safely from all harm,
   To waters sweet and clear—
   A spring of water in the man
   Of hope, and love and fear.

4 Salvation! O our thoughts revive,
   To press with vigor on,
   Until we shall the bliss receive,
   By a kind Saviour won.

NO. 253. S. M.

1 GRACE like a river flows,
   From heavenly fields above,
   Whose healing waters, ever glows
   With faith, and hope, and love.

2 Grace scents these earthly minds,
   That heavenly fruit may bring;
   Happy, the soul, that ever finds
   Whence the rich treasures spring.

3 The fruit will ripen fast,
    Unfolding every hour,
  Sweet to the soul of heavenly taste,
    Composed of love and power.

4 We'll raise our thoughts to scan
    From whence this grace proceeds,
  View Him who caused salvation's plan,
    Our hope and zeal provides.

5 Grace shall complete the whole,
    And well deserves the praise
  Of richest strains from every soul,
    Preserved for heavenly days.

NO. 254. C. M.

1 AH! prophecy! who struck thee now?
    Thou Christ, King of the Jews!
  While kindred friends in silence stood,
    Nor dared to interpose.

2 How dreadful is the thought, to think
    This was the Prince of Peace!
  While sinners standing on the brink,
  Filled their law, room and place.

3 With all the scorns man could invent,
    Was put upon Him here,
  While God through him salvation sent,
    Through Him our hopes appear.

4 No guile in Him was ever found,
    The spotless Lamb of God,
  While man in ruined cells was bound,
    In crimes of dark abode.

5 O, could we hide our weeping eyes,
   When we behold the scene,
  Our gracious Lord, though once despised,
   Has brought redemption down.

6 Yes, through Him hangs a living vail,
   To hide our every sin—
  Through Him our God designs to hail,
   And bring His children in.

NO. 255.   C. M.

1 COULD I but view the eternal love
   On mortals here bestowed
  By Jesus from the courts above,
   Whose blood in rivers flowed;

2 Could I but claim the promise sure
   To this poor wandering heart,
  I would these conflicts here endure,
   Under the rending smart.

3 Nature is weak, and soon must fall;
   O may that love be mine—
  My hope, my comfort, and my all,
   Eternal and divine.

4 Impart that grace within my heart,
   Dear Jesus, now, I pray,
  While sin of every grade depart,
   E'er in Thy courts I stay.

5 And when this heart and flesh shall fail,
   O may I there possess
  A life of joy within the vail,
   Of perfect love and peace.

THE WANDERING PILGRIM.

NO. 256. P. M.

1 'MID scenes of sorrow.
And confusion I roam,
And long for the morrow,
To arrive at that boon,
Where trouble no more
Shall my soul e'er distress,
But live with my Master
In realms of His bliss.

2 Speed on lively now,
Rolling wheels—bring the day
When Jesus my Lord
Shall convey me away
To mansions prepared,
Where His children shall rest,
In the courts of His beauty,
The paradise blest.

3 O'erwhelmed with anguish,
I have here no joy;
The world, sin and Satan
My hopes quite destroy;
But now and then I see
A small glimmering ray,
That heaven's not distant—
O haste on the day!

4 There, doubts, fears and toiling,
With me soon shall cease,
While envy and hatred
No more shall molest;
And Jesus shall smile
All my sorrows away,
While singing and praising
Shall be my employ.

THE WANDERING PILGRIM. 235

NO. 257. P. M.

1 CLOSE by Bethesda's pool
   The mourning captives lay,
And none to help them in,
   Though toiling all the day ;
But for the want of some kind aid,
The impotent man a long while laid.

2 At length the Saviour comes—
   How soon his hopes did rise !—
Behold ! salvation reigns
   In the Redeemer's eyes.
Come, leave the pool, all hopes despair—
No one can help thee even there.

3 The law obedience claim—
   How can we walk therein,
When we are blind and lame,
   And all defiled with sin ?
And for the want of nobler skill,
Like the impotent man we fail.

4 The sinner long will try,
   Until all hopes do fail,
And given up to die,
   For mercy hear him wail:
Dear Lord, have mercy on my soul !
O, canst Thou make the sinner whole ?

5 Take up thy bed and walk,
   The blest Redeemer said ;
Unloosed his tongue to talk,
   And tell how long he laid.
Although it was these many years,
The Saviour quelled his vital fears.

NO. 258. S. M.

1 O, HEAVENLY spirit! come
  Dwell in this mortal breast;
Peaceful may I reposing in
  Thee, as my sacred rest.

2 Supported from Thy hand,
  I live from day to day;
O, for a heart to tender Thee
  My life, my all, I pray.

3 In every thing I do,
  Thy goodness I implore,
Confirm my footsteps here below,
  And line them for that shore.

4 Where fears and sorrows driven
  Far from the peaceful breast
Of him who gains that glorious heaven,
  The sacred place of rest.

NO. 259.

1 HEAVENLY dove! celestial spirit!
  Come and dwell in this poor heart;
Ought have I to plead for merit—
  Wealth or greatness I have not;
In the world I've sought for treasure—
  Nothing have I found but pain;
Banished every peaceful pleasure,
  To increase a little gain.

2 Come! O come! heaven's adoring—
  With Thee am I ever blest;
Come! O come! and give me hearing—
  Without Thee I cannot rest.

Fill my heart with heaven's blessing,
Teach me where my treasures lay,
In Thee, pleasures never ceasing—
Condescend with me to stay.

3 Come! O come! and cease my toiling,
Striving at the heavenly gate;
May I see my joys arising,
While for Thee I hungering wait.
Come! O come! and cheer my dwelling
With beams of heavenly rays;
Come! O come! my bosom swelling
With hopes of brighter days.

4 Are my sorrows e'er subsiding?
Shall I ever see Thy love?
Shall I reach that place abiding,
Raised for heavenly joys above?
O, confirm my sins forgiven,
Constantly my hopes annoy,
Spreading forth to hide that heaven
Where is all my real joy.

NO. 260.   C. M.

1 FREED from the pangs of sin and death,
Let anxious cares be still;
The Lord has cheered our latest breath,
To do His sovereign will.

2 Nature is blind and cannot read—
Why should such joys arise?
While the poor soul, whose sins are freed,
Looks on beyond the skies.

3 There looks through an immortal birth,
From whence these blessings flow,

And fills up this poor mortal earth,
And makes a heaven below.

4 Nature, with all her noise and show,
Can't imitate such love,
As heaven's heirs have seen below,
A glimpse of that above.

5 Nature must soon dissolve and fall
Back to her mother dust;
While God shall His dear children call,
And raise them with the just.

6 There shall we in perfection shine,
Bright as the orbs of light,
Till God shall change this earth of mine,
And raise from shades of night.

7 United in that glorious morn,
Whose sun is ever risen,
The victory shall our King adorn,
For the bright scenes of heaven.

NO. 261. S. M.

1 WHAT wandering minds to rove,
We mortals have below!
Forsaking Him our souls approved,
And raised us from our woe.

2 At war with God we stood,
Condemned in sin and shame,
Our sorrows rolled in like a flood,
And banishment proclaimed.

3 Jesus in pity stood,
A wavering voice exclaimed,

"Come, follow me—the way is good—
Ye halt, and blind, and lame."

4 Leaping and praising God,
   What stammering tongues can tell,
Our Saviour, by a sovereign word,
   Our deadly wounds made well.

5 Why should we e'er forget
   His mercies to proclaim?
Amazing love, come warm the heart,
   That we may love that name.

NO. 262.   7s.

1 DARK and doleful was the night,
Doom'd the Son of God's delight,
There exposed to sin and shame,
He who never was to blame.

2 While if justice rightly felled
'Twould have sunk us down to hell.
But the surety bore the stroke;
Bless the Lord for such a hope.

3 Could my soul dare ever claim
Jesus thought on my poor name,
When the captives He did free
Lost and ruined men like me.

4 Wondrous love, the mighty God,
Vail'd like us in flesh and blood,
To exonerate our case
He himself supplied our place.

5 O, for love to praise His name,
He has washed away our stain,
Given a hope that all is well,
Though 'tis marvelous to tell.

6 Come, dear saints, and shed one tear
   Over such a heavenly bier;
   Through His death and risen rays
   Every hope of promise lays.

NO. 263.   C. M.

1 Let all our tongues and all our thoughts
   Be fixed to raise a song
   Of adoration to the Lord
   For all His mercies shown.

2 Through every period of our life
   Behold His wondrous care,
   Emerged in sin and shame and strife,
   Stained all our comforts were.

3 But He appeared, obedience given,
   That raised our drooping heads,
   And made an entrance to yon heaven
   Where all our glories spread.

4 Through Him what tongues can ever tell
   The beams of great surprise;
   May our hosannas constant swell
   Our great Redeemer's praise.

NO. 264.   C. M.

1 IN everything befalls us here
   We'll look to Providence,
   Our guard and our protector true,
   A rock of sure defense.

2 Troubles and trials by the way,
   Like mountains seem to rise,
   But as we journey on they view
   As bubbles in disguise.

3 Nor shall our fears ever prevail
   While God defends our way,
His goodness shall our foes assail,
   And turn our fears to joy.

4 His hands the rich provision spread,
   And bids us to the feast;
It lies beyond these lower skies
   O'r many a stormy blast.

5 Were not for the protection given
   Where would our hopes appear;
Beneath the howling tempest driven,
   And lost in keen despair.

6 But faith anticipates the day,
   Confirmed by every dawn,
Methinks I hear the angels say,
   Awake ye lovely morn.

7 Awake ye morn whose sun ne'er sets,
   And bring the wishful day,
Where every shadow of a doubt
   Shall sink beneath thy ray.

8 O, glorious hope, O bless'd abode,
   From storms of sorrow free'd,
Dress'd in the image of our God,
   What more could wish or need.

NO. 265. S. M.

1 LET all creation bring
   Upon their Maker's nod,
The music of the joys that spring,
   And fills His vast abode.

2 Our life and health and strength
   His wisdom does supply,
While through mandates of His will
   Our active fears defy.

3 Our strife and fear comes from
   Our disobedience here,
Amid the billows heaving storm
   Our sins and guilt appear.

4 Forsaken'd and cast down,
   Our hopes shall rise again,
Supplied with grace in every form,
   O'er sin and guilt shall reign.

5 The brightness of that day
   The illumined sun outshines,
Happy the soul whose form obey,
   And on his God reclines.

6 Whose precepts to obey,
   The injunctions are divine,
Brings night and darkness into day,
   Where hope and mercy shine.

7 Our disobedience fills
   The heart with fear and gloom,
While o'er our hopes our fears prevail,
   Brings darkness out of noon.

8 O, let our hearts obey
   His early, only choice,
And from that midnight darkness flee,
   Attend the heavenly voice.

9 The Christian mind shall roam
   O'er pastures bright and green,
In the obedience of that form
   From the beginning seen.

10 Let every creature now
   Obey your Maker's nod,
 In all His precepts reverence show
   That we do love the Lord.

NO. 266.　　C. M.

1 HOW solemn yet how fair it is
   To dwell at Jesus' feet,
 While the bright rays of heavenly dews
   Fall round the mercy seat.

2 'Tis there my sweetest joys arise,
   'Tis there my sorrows wane,
 While every heart and tongue employs
   To spread the Saviour's name.

3 Amazing wonder spread the feast,
   For dying souls 'tis given,
 While saints shall bid the invited guest
   To taste the joys of heaven.

4 Why was I made to feel that love
   Of faith and hope and zeal,
 And seek those joys prepared above
   Upon Mount Zion's Hill.

5 'Twas the same love that made the room,
   The invitation given,
 Else had still engage to roam,
   And scanned the road to heaven.

6 O, may my choicest songs arise,
   O, may my sorrows flow,
 And swell that name with weeping eyes
   That makes these hopes to grow.

NO. 267.   S. M.

1 RELIGION, how divine,
   To mortals here below;
  'Twill fit them for that heavenly shrine
   Where all its virtues grow.

2 'Twill sweeten life's sorrow
   On every turning page,
  And O, the joys that will follow
   In the declining age.

3 No pen can e'er describe
   On this terrestrial ball;
  Religion is the Christian's guide,
   His God, his heaven his all.

NO. 268.   P. M.

1 WHO is the Prince of Peace?
   Come, tell me, dearest friend,
  That I may taste His grace,
   A hope and pardon find.
  I'd leave the world with all its charms,
  And fall in my dear Jesus' arms.

2 Like Simeon of old,
   The child he freely blest,
  Thy servant now is bold,
   And will depart in peace.
  To see Thy great salvation, Lord,
  Secures my hope a free reward.

3 I would depart in peace,
   Could I behold Thy face;
  O, bid my journey cease,
   Thou God of righteousness.

And while I live from day to day,
O, may I ever live to Thee.

4 When sighs and sorrows o'er,
A hope of promised rest,
Will stimulate to endure,
And lean upon Thy breast.
Though troubles roll and fears oppress,
I'll drop them with this dying flesh.

NO. 269. L. M.

1 BLESS, O my soul, thou God of peace,
Call home my thoughts that rove abroad,
And through Thy all abounding grace
Teach me Thy goodness to applaud.

2 My thoughts are drifting like the snow
On objects of no real worth,
While nature shuns Thy name to know,
Engaged to love the things of earth.

3 In vain I strive with earthly zeal
To raise one note of heavenly praise,
My heart insensible as steel,
O, for the dawn of nobler days.

4 O, for the dawn, when I shall see
No roving thoughts, no chilling winds,
From every sin and sorrow free,
Borne to that heavenly spirit land.

5 No tears to wipe, no foes to fear,
No rambling thoughts to jar my notes;
But in His image shall appear
Who has engaged my warmest thoughts.

NO. 270. L. M.

1 THERE is a period known to God,
   When the poor sinner, dead in sin,
Shall lay his works of art aside,
   Turn to the fold and enter in.

2 Though foes annoy and fears oppress,
   He shall attend the quickening voice;
The Lord shall heal up his distress,
   And own him favorite of His choice.

3 The Lord shall make His glories known,
   Without the charms of mortal aid;
He gives command, and all must own
   The sinner's in the balance weighed.

4 He views his case is dark indeed,
   Without the Lord should interfere,
His prayers no higher than his head
   Can go, while justice smites with fear.

5 Acknowledged justice he must own,
   E'er should the Lord send down to hell.
While mercy cries from justice's throne,
   Here's pardon, marvelous to tell.

6 O come, my son, the Lord replies,
   I have this day begotten thee;
Dismiss thy fears, I've heard thy cries,
   Thy sins are all forgiven thee.

7 'Tis thus the Lord works out His will,
   And man can't tell the reason why,
That some are brought to Zion's hill,
   Whilst other souls are left to die.

8 Secure in our esteem we stand,
   And think we do His precepts fill;

But how mistaken'd shall we find,
Unless revealed in His will.

9 We pray Thy will in us be done,
The image of Thy heavenly name,
Reserved and kept e'er through Thy Son,
A glorious hope, strong to redeem.

10 Strong to redeem and born to save,
The objects of Thy wondrous grace,
While sinners shall be taught to love,
And serve the Lord, our righteousness.

NO. 271.   L. M.

1 MY troubles like a darkened cloud,
Have gathered thick and thundered loud,
And should they break upon my head,
May blessings come out of the dread.

2 The Lord is my protector, guide,
And to His will I must abide;
If He sees fit to punish me,
I must endure, I cannot flee.

3 His presence fills immensity,
His power is equal to his day;
But O, His love could I dare claim,
I'd fear not all the powers of men.

4 Could I but say my sins forgiven,
The glorious thought to dream of heav'n;
Joined with the kindred souls of bliss,
Where trouble ne'er can break my peace.

NO. 272. S. M.

1 WHAT charming thoughts compose,
  Salvation's ever free,
And like a river ever flows
  In streams of equity.

2 Viewed in our natural head,
  We sons of Adam lay,
Without one hope to reinstead
  Or bring a welcome day.

3 Yea, dead to all that's good,
  Stung by the law of sin,
To flee from danger where we stood,
  Combined the thoughts within.

4 Beyond the reach of hope
  Was grace in mercy sent,
When justice, with uplifted stroke,
  Portraying banishment.

5 Grace, like a guided dart,
  Surveyed my inmost thought;
While in my heart the promise wrote,
  And all my sorrows took.

6 Constrained by grace we sing,
  Our sins are all forgiven,
While grace to us the promise brings,
  Unvails the hopes of heaven.

NO. 273. 4s, 6s.

1 THE cause of Heaven,
  The loveliest cause to man,
    Whose sins forgiven,
  Through Him, the sinner's friend.

2   Redeemed from weal,
    For that eternal day,
        O, could I feel,
        The great surprising ray,

3   Where kindred meet
    To sing redeeming grace,
        Communion sweet,
        Joined in the bonds of peace.

4   Join the chorus—
    Let all our voices raise
        Hallelujahs
        To sing our Saviour's praise.

NO. 274.   P. M.

1   SWEET flowers of Paradise,
        Celestial fruits will bring,
    And heavenly minds suffice
        To eat, and drink, and sing ;
    For plants revived by living grace,
    Bring fruits of joy, and love and peace.

2   These flowers on earthly ground,
        Will never yield their fruit,
    For nature's soil is bound
        With sin, and shame, and guilt ;
    But plants revived by living grace,
    Bring fruits of joy, and love, and peace.

3   God has salvation sent
        To earthly minds below,
    Straightened the twig, 'twas bent,
        And gave a heavenly hue.
    The plants revived by living grace,
    Bring fruits of joy, and love, and peace.

NO. 275.

FAREWELL.

1 I MUST this volume close—
   Its pages are now full;
Should you ne'er hear my voice again,
   Be not astonished, friend.

2 A wandering mind I have,
   And more than all, a heart
Ungrateful to the God I love,
   Insensible in part.

3 That part will soon decay,
   Fast hastening to the grave—
Submissive to my God, obey,
   My nobler powers will save.

4 Before I bid farewell,
   Dear friends, remember me;
In many sorrows I've befell,
   A wandering pilgrim be.

5 Now, if I've said amiss,
   Contrary to the Word,
O, who will pardon works like these?
   I trust I will be heard.

6 May he who faults my word,
   Be careful where he stand;
I'm on my journey, long for home,
   To my Emanuel's land.

7 To fairer world's on high,
   I feel assured to go,
Where Jesus reigns the God of day,
   Beyond all sorrows too.

8 Now farewell, my dear friends,
    Farewell poor sinners too,
  I'll leave you in Jehovah's hands,
    Who will His pleasures do.

9 To bring you conquerors home,
    Through wisdom truth and grace,
  To see our capitol's high dome,
    There see our God in peace.

www.ingramcontent.com/pod-product-compliance
Lightning Source LLC
Chambersburg PA
CBHW032138230426
43672CB00011B/2384